In Deuteronomy 30:19, God tells us, "I ha
death, blessings and curses. Now choose life, so that you and your
children may live." Dave Sterrett's must-read book, *We Choose Life*,
illuminates the truth of that Scripture by profiling courageous individuals who are making a profound life-saving impact. The stories that fill
the pages of *We Choose Life* demonstrate that we should not wait for
politicians or judges to end abortion. It is up to you and me, and we
can't underestimate what one person can do. One person—answering
the call to "speak up for those who cannot speak for themselves"—can
transform a campus, a neighborhood, a city, a state, our nation . . . and
the entire world. Read *We Choose Life* today and discover how God
can work through YOU to save lives!

David Bereit, National Director of 40 Days for Life

The ethical pro-life position must be one that takes into account all
the complexities and perspectives surrounding the abortion debate in
our time. This book comes closer to this fullness of perspective than
any book I have read on the subject. *We Choose Life* gathers together
diverse voices of reason, compassion, experience, and knowledge to
offer one life-affirming symphony.

**Karen Swallow Prior, PhD, author of *Booked: Literature in
the Soul of Me* and *Fierce Convictions: The Extraordinary
Life of Hannah More: Poet, Reformer, Abolitionist***

The Bible reminds us that in Jesus Christ, "the light shines in the darkness, and the darkness has not overcome it" (John 1:5). Dave Sterrett's
book *We Choose Life* reminds Christians that truth will continue to
make significant inroads into the darkness of abortion so long as God's
people continue to stand with principle, compassion, and conviction.

Jim Daly, President of Focus on the Family

The word "epic" is way over-used in our bubble gum culture today. However, "epic" is the word that grabbed my heart when I read *We Choose Life*. The safest place in the world for a baby should be a mother's womb. Sadly, in America, and the majority of the world, endangered species are more protected than precious, helpless babies. The "right to choose" is denying someone else "the right to live." In the pages of this book, you will find the hope of Jesus, the forgiveness of Jesus, and the heart of Jesus.

> **Derwin L. Gray, Lead Pastor, Transformation Church,**
> **and author of *Limitless Life: You Are More Than***
> ***Your Past When God Holds Your Future***

We Choose Life is a great encouragement to all pro-life advocates as well as a resource for those struggling with the debate. Dave Sterrett has compiled a compelling group of stories that show the true pain and heartache that surround abortion, and I am grateful for his efforts in producing such an encouraging book of stories.

> **Charmaine Yoest, PhD, Americans United for Life**

There are many important books that make the intellectual case for protecting preborn human life. You'll find the core elements of that case in *We Choose Life*. What makes this book different is that the contributors follow the model of Jesus in the Gospels: they tell compelling and sometimes heart-breaking stories that show, as profoundly as any argument, the dignity of human life at its most vulnerable. I pray that this book helps shine a bright light in the enveloping dark of the culture of death.

> **Jay W. Richards, PhD, assistant research professor,**
> **The Catholic University of America, and *New York Times***
> **bestselling author of *Infiltrated* and *Indivisible***

We Choose Life addresses the evil of abortion but more importantly shows hope for this fight for life and human dignity. The tide is turning in America on this issue and I am so grateful to my friend Dave for speaking up for the defenseless. Spread the message of life through this fantastic book.

> **Sujo John, founder of YouCanFree.Us**

I'm so grateful for Dave Sterrett's decision to be a voice for the voice-less. We need more resources like this that help Christians engage the important cultural issues of our day. As you read this book, you will be challenged to fight for the life of the preborn and speak out on their behalf.

Jack Graham, Pastor, Prestonwood Baptist Church

The momentum of the pro-life movement just went into hyper-drive! History will record Dave Sterrett's book *We Choose Life* as the booster fuel to victory. Casual voters "for" pro-life just got yanked off their couches to be "with" pro-life. Get the blue and pink balloons ready because a bunch of babies are about to have their birthday!

Tony Nolan, author and evangelist

Abortion is partially hidden by deceptive language and complicit media outlets that refuse to expose it. No more. In this book are the stories that need to be told about abortion, from a variety of angles. But beware: anyone who reads it will never again be able to say, "But I didn't know . . ."

John Stonestreet, radio voice for *BreakPoint* and Fellow of the Chuck Colson Center for Christian Worldview

It is not a cliché to say that the pro-life movement is about hearts and minds—it's true, all you have to do is look inside the movement. The people you encounter in these pages had different paths but all of them shed light on how much closer we are to seeing an abortion-free America.

Shawn Carney, National Campaign Director, 40 Days for Life, and co-author of *40 Days for Life*

We Choose Life is not some faddish book of the hour but a biblical mandate and the clarion call of the century. President Reagan was right when he said, "I've noticed that everyone who is for abortion has already been born." Read this book and let this book read you. Share with others and may we cease being content with nothing less than promoting life, liberty, and every right to the pursuit of happiness.

Frank Shelton Jr., Evangelism Chairman, 2012 and 2016 Olympics Outreach (LWFCI), and Fox News contributor

Nothing evil and entrenched in the world can be overcome except with exceptional determination and ability. I see both of these characteristics in the ministry of Dave Sterrett, one of America's leading young pro-life voices. Dave, a man of deep faith and formidable intellect, has authored a book that promises to push the cause of human dignity further ahead. The courageous narratives in this book are not for display purposes, however. They are catalysts that will engage us, move us, and ultimately drive us from the sidelines into the heart of the greatest cause of our day.

Owen Strachan, PhD, author of *Risky Gospel: Abandon Fear and Build Something Awesome,* and President of the Council on Biblical Manhood and Womanhood

We Choose Life is sure to encourage, challenge, and perhaps even disrupt some preconceived ideas of all who read it. The most captivating facet of *We Choose Life* is the breadth of the perspectives from which its stories are taken, from the adoptee, to the ex-abortionist, to teens impassioned to expose the lies, to post-abortive women and men—even a pastor's son—to children born with disabilities or conceived through rape. Like the facets of a bright star in a dark night, each story shines forth as a glorious point in a multifaceted display, coming together in one powerful declaration: that all life is precious and every life is a priceless gift from our loving Creator.

Shadia Hrichi, pro-life speaker, teacher, and author of *Worthy of Love: A Journey of Hope and Healing after Abortion*

What you hold in your hands may be one of the most important books you'll ever read. Sterrett writes from a place of anguish and utilizes stories, statistics, Scripture and a humble sensitivity in this book. I'm thankful for Dave's riveting wake-up call to be a voice for the voiceless. To choose life!

Dr. Bobby Conway, Lead Pastor, Life Fellowship Church, and founder of The One Minute Apologist

WE
CHOOSE
Life

WE CHOOSE *Life*

AUTHENTIC STORIES | *Movements of Hope*

DAVE STERRETT
GENERAL EDITOR

with contributions from Ramona Treviño,
Mike Adams, Rebecca Kiessling, Kristan Hawkins,
Melissa Ohden, Scott Klusendorf, and more

HENDRICKSON
PUBLISHERS

We Choose Life: Authentic Stories, Movements of Hope

© 2016 Hendrickson Publishers Marketing, LLC
P. O. Box 3473
Peabody, Massachusetts 01961-3473

ISBN 978-1-61970-762-7

Printed in the United States of America

First Printing—January 2016

Library of Congress Cataloging-in-Publication Data

A catalog record for this book is available from the Library of Congress

Hendrickson Publishers Marketing, LLC ISBN 978-1-61970-762-7

Contents

~

Introduction—A Voice for the Voiceless

Dave Sterrett

On a cool October day, Angela Balderaz, a Hispanic woman in her early twenties, stood near me outside Southwestern Women's Surgical Center, an abortion facility off Greenville Avenue in Dallas. She was not there to have an abortion, but to be a voice of hope and to share her story with those of us who were praying outside the facility. About one hundred of us had gathered that fall day across the street from the clinic. We sang worship songs and read Scriptures. Some held signs that read "Pray to end abortion" and "Choose Life." We were Protestants and Catholics, elders and youths, families and single people. We weren't there to yell or condemn. We were there to pray that abortion would end in our city.

Angela stepped forward on a podium and began to speak. She told the crowd, "My story, like everyone's story, began in the womb. My biological mother was a woman of the streets, a prostitute. My father was a well-known drug dealer in the city of Dallas in the 1980s. My mother conceived a child and she chose to go to an abortion facility to have an abortion. But as days passed after the procedure, something did not feel right. She felt a baby moving in her womb, and my mom took matters into her own hands. She increased heavy drug and alcohol use hoping that her baby would not survive. Even so, on June 6, 1987, she went into labor and I was born."

God had protected Angela. I could sense God's power on Angela's life. She continued, "About a year passed, and my mom conceived again. My little sister Alysia was born, and she had to stay in the hospital longer than normal because of the influence of my mother's use of cocaine and heroin. Two weeks after my parents eventually brought Alysia home, they killed her. It was a homicide. They fled the scene, and I was found after being left alone for about a week—alone but for the corpse of my sister. To this day we are still not sure who contacted the police, but the police came to the apartment and rescued me. I was in filthy living conditions, with a very dirty diaper on a bare, stained mattress and no food in the entire house."

I thought about what an evil and hypocritical world we live in. Angela's birth parents were rightly charged with homicide for the death of Alysia. But if Angela's birth parents had aborted her sister mere weeks earlier while she was still in the womb, their actions would have been protected and even celebrated by some Americans who would have claimed that killing Alysia before birth was justified in the name of "women's rights" or "women's health."

Angela continued speaking. "They took me to Child Protective Services and tried to match me with family members. But no one could afford to take me. I was put in the custody of my biological grandmother, and she put me up for adoption because she was dying from a brain tumor. My grandmother requested that I be placed in a Christian family who followed the ways of God. Two weeks after I was put in her custody, my grandmother died. Despite her wish that I be adopted, I traveled the foster care system for the next year and half, living in what were not the best of conditions.

"Two years later a couple, Victor and Maxine, were contacted for the possibility of adopting me. Maxine was sterile. They had tried fertility shots and other methods but could not conceive, so they had decided to adopt. Child Protective Services told them that I had been diagnosed with muteness, because I would not respond to certain testing and could not talk even at the age of three. Maxine and Victor still wanted to adopt me.

"When they went to the agency to adopt me, the social worker told Maxine, 'She's your daughter now. What would you like to name her?' Maxine replied, 'I want to name her Angela, because she's like an angel, a gift from God.' The social worker started tearing up and said, 'Ma'am, that was her original name, Angela.' Maxine and Victor rejoiced with tears of happiness as they thanked God and brought me into their home."

God had intervened in darkness to rescue Angela. As I thought about her story, I prayed that God would somehow intervene to rescue other children from abortion at the facility right in front of us. Jesus temporarily permits evils in this world because he has given human beings a free will, but sometimes I wish he would destroy all evil. But I know that if God did that, he would have to destroy all of mankind because of the evil we have done. Although our evil deeds may not match some criminals' actions, we have still fallen short of God's moral standards.

Angela went on, "Maxine and Victor took me in and loved me. They poured themselves into my life and soon I began talking. It became clear that I could also hear and respond. The diagnosis of my muteness was a mistake. Later, by God's grace, I excelled in school. Also, about two years later, my mother Maxine became pregnant and gave birth to my brother Jonathan. She later gave birth to two more boys. Her apparent sterility may have been a misdiagnosis, but I believe it was God's intervention to bless my parent's faithfulness. My story is confirmation that God is sovereign. He is in control."

I fought back tears as I thought about God's overwhelming grace in Angela's life. But I also knew that at that very hour, baby boys and girls were going to be killed. Unlike Angela, they would never have the opportunity to be adopted.

Angela's story is one of many incredible stories that I have encountered in recent years as I have thrown myself into the pro-life movement. In this book, I want to introduce you to remarkable individuals like Angela: people who demonstrate the importance of fighting for the right to life.

On the day that I heard Angela speak, I sensed spiritual warfare as we stood outside Southwestern Women's Surgical Center. The facility was originally established by abortionist Dr. Curtis Boyd, a man credited with being the first physician to open a legal abortion clinic in Texas after the Supreme Court ruling on *Roe v. Wade* on January 22, 1973. He was involved in establishing the National Abortion Federation, and he remains unapologetic for his work. When Texas television news station KVUE interviewed him in 2009, Boyd said to the interviewer, "Am I killing? Yes, I am. I know that. . . . I'm an ordained Baptist minister." After performing abortions, he said, "I'll ask that the spirit of [the] pregnancy be returned to God with love and with understanding."[1]

My heart broke for those preborn children when I first saw Dr. Boyd speak these words in an online version of the interview. I knew that his falsely "spiritual" prayers were actually demonic. The very act of killing an innocent human being could only be encouraged by the evil one. Jesus said, "The thief comes only to steal and kill and destroy. I came that they may have life and have it abundantly" (John 10:10 ESV). Satan has always hated life, especially the vulnerable lives of children. Herod tried to destroy the baby boys of Bethlehem at the time of Christ's birth, but an angel warned Joseph in a dream to escape to Egypt.

This was not the first time in Israel's history when the lives of its children had been threatened. When God was delivering the Hebrew people out of slavery in Egypt, Pharaoh commanded that all male Hebrew children be killed. The slaughter was averted by some seemingly ordinary people—the Hebrew midwives, who "feared God" and secretly disobeyed Pharaoh's order (Exod 1:17). In those dangerous times, a courageous young Levite family also disobeyed Pharaoh and protected their baby, Moses, by placing him in a basket in the marsh alongside the Nile River. Moses's sister kept an eye on her baby brother and made sure that he was protected until, eventually, he was found and adopted by Pharaoh's own daughter. When he was a young adult, Moses could have continued to live in the comfort of Pharaoh's household, but he chose not to, actually refusing to be called the son of Pharaoh's daughter. By living in obedience to God, Moses was able to deliver the people of Israel out of slavery. When Moses was one hundred and twenty years old and about to die, his last message to the people of Israel was, "Choose life." The book of Deuteronomy records his final message:

> Today I have given you the choice between life and death, between blessings and curses. Now I call on heaven and earth to witness the choice you make. *Oh, that you would choose life*, so that you and your descendants might live! You can make this choice by loving the LORD your God, obeying him, and committing yourself firmly to him. (Deut 30:19–20 NLT)

Throughout the ages, there has always been a spiritual battle to diminish the dignity of certain groups of people, and to *choose death*. When acts of evil were carried out against certain people, those acts weren't only being done in some distant land, but close to the neighborhoods and cities of good people who were living busy lives. The political philosopher Edmund Burke is often cited as saying, "The only thing necessary for the triumph of evil is for good men to do nothing." For the longest time, I did very little for the unborn. I thought that, as a man, there was very little I could do.

That attitude reminds me of an account from a church member in Nazi Germany. Put yourself in the shoes of these Germans and ask, "What would *I* have done?"

> I lived in Germany during the Nazi Holocaust. I considered myself a Christian. We heard stories of what was happening to the Jews, but we tried to distance ourselves from it, because, what could anyone do to stop it?

A railroad track ran behind our small church and each Sunday morning we could hear the whistle in the distance and then the wheels coming over the tracks. We became disturbed when we heard the cries coming from the train as it passed by. We realized that it was carrying Jews like cattle in the cars!

Week after week the whistle would blow. We dreaded to hear the sound of those wheels because we knew that we would hear the cries of the Jews en route to a death camp. Their screams tormented us.

We knew the time the train was coming and when we heard the whistle blow we began singing hymns. By the time the train came past our church we were singing at the top of our voices. If we heard the screams, we sang more loudly and soon we heard them no more.

Years have passed and no one talks about it anymore. But I still hear that train whistle in my sleep. God forgive me; forgive all of us who called ourselves Christians yet did nothing to intervene.[2]

What would *I* have done? Would I have kept singing and tried to ignore the cries? Would I have had the attitude, "There's nothing I can do about it"? As an evangelist, would I have kept quiet and told myself, "I don't want to get political, because I'm just focused on the gospel"? *Or would I have done something?*

How many times have we gathered in our churches, while at the same time, just a couple miles away, babies are being slaughtered? Yet we rarely mention it or seem to care. We just keep singing like the Christians who ignored the crying Jews en route to the death camps.

Don't get me wrong, we *should* sing songs to God, and sing with enthusiasm. But sadly, we sometimes we get so caught up with our own lives, and with trying not to offend society, that we neglect the very "least of these," the babies who are being aborted in our own communities. The Bible says:

Rescue those being led away to death; hold back those staggering toward slaughter. If you say, "But we knew nothing about this," does not he who weighs the heart perceive it? Does not he who guards your life know it? Will he not repay everyone according to what they have done? (Prov 24:11–12)

This verse reminds me that as a follower of Jesus, we actually need to *rescue* the innocent who are being led to death. And we cannot use ignorance as an excuse. When we ignore children who are being led away to be slaughtered at Planned Parenthood, we are ignoring Jesus, who said, "I tell you the truth, when you refused to help the least of these . . . you were refusing to help me" (Matt 25:45 NLT). Jesus also said, "Whoever welcomes one of these little children in my name welcomes me" (Mark 9:37).

A few years ago, around the time that I was being convicted in my own heart to do something, I ran into my friend Carmen Pate at a coffee shop. (Carmen's story appears in Chapter 5.) I knew that she was pro-life because she had hosted a Christian radio show that frequently talked about the sacredness of human life. I said, "Carmen, I need your help. I'm pro-life, but as a man, I don't know how I can get involved. Do you know of any ways that I can volunteer to help rescue babies and families from abortion?" She smiled and said, "Yes!" She began telling me about two men, David Bereit and Shawn Carney, who had started a prayer movement called 40 Days for Life in Bryan, Texas. As a result of people praying outside the local Planned Parenthood, the manager of the abortion facility, Abby Johnson, quit her job and eventually joined 40 Days for Life. Carmen had served on the 40 Days for Life non-profit organizational board and told me that thousands of volunteers around the world were joining the prayer movement, praying outside abortion facilities. Carmen asked me if, in a few months, I would fly to Washington, D.C., to serve on the national board of 40 Days for Life and attend the March for Life in our nation's capital. I told her, "Absolutely!"

Although I was excited to fly to Washington, D.C., I also wanted to get involved at a local level in Dallas. I searched on the Internet for "Pro-Life Dallas," and I made a phone call to an organization called the Catholic Pro-Life Committee, which was involved with the local 40 Days for Life chapter. Four women involved with the local prayer outreach group in Dallas met me for lunch. One of the women, Lauren Muzyka (whose story also appears in this book), told me about sidewalk counseling. When a young woman walks into an abortion center, there are just a few seconds to offer help and to point out that she can receive free medical counseling—including pregnancy tests and sonograms—if she walks across the street with you to a pregnancy counseling center.

Lauren said that women are often brought to abortion clinics by their husbands or boyfriends, and that male sidewalk counselors are needed to talk to these men. This was something I could do. So one Saturday morning I drove by Lamar Robinson's Abortion Advantage in Dallas. Students from the nearby Catholic college, the University of Dallas, were already praying on the sidewalk outside the abortion clinic. As I exited my car and approached them, I felt nervous and, honestly, a little afraid. One of the students recognized me because I was enrolled as a part-time graduate student in philosophy at the University of Dallas. We shook hands, and after talking briefly about our class on St. Augustine's *Confessions*, I quietly admitted that even though I was pro-life, I had never prayed outside an abortion clinic before. He was kind and asked me to join them in the Lord's Prayer.

After we prayed, I stood and watched a young couple get out of their car and walk toward the abortion facility. One of the Catholic students spoke up, "Before you go in there, can I please help you?" The boyfriend smirked and gave us the middle finger. An elderly lady held out a small brochure and calmly said to the young lady, "We just want to help you receive all the options. Across the street, you can receive free pregnancy testing and medical services." The girl took the brochure, but her boyfriend continued holding his middle finger up as they entered the clinic.

As the clinic door shut behind them, I felt helpless. The weight of their abortion was on my heart. I wanted to rescue that young lady and her baby. I felt angry toward the young man, but I remembered the words of Christ, "Love your enemies, bless them that curse you, do good to them that hate you, and pray for them which despitefully use you" (Matt 5:44 KJV). I prayed quietly that God would change their minds.

As the hours passed, I watched a steady stream of young women enter the abortion facility. The abortion clinic's guard escorted women and their companions across the street to try to insulate them from our words. At one point, I addressed him, "Hi, I'm Dave. What's your name?" He told me his name. I then asked him if I could help him find another job. He laughed and said, "No, Dr. Lamar has been good to me. He takes me to NBA games. He gets me great tickets." I asked the man, "Do you believe in God?" He said, "Yes. I'm a Christian." I responded, "Do you remember when Jesus said, 'What profit is it for a man if he gains the whole world, yet forfeits his soul?' Is that a risk that you are willing to take?" The guard looked away and said, "Dave, it's not that simple. I've talked to my pastor about this. It's tough, but my relationship with God is personal. I have to go." "It's not just personal," I replied. "Your actions influence other people." He walked back to the abortion facility.

Soon after, I watched a nurse push a young woman in a wheelchair back to her car. Soon after, I watched a nurse walk alongside another woman who had also just had an abortion. The pain on the faces of these women was real. One girl was in tears. The other looked dazed. My heart ached as I left the prayer vigil and returned to my car. I fought back tears as I drove away, and I began to pray the words of Christ, "Father, forgive them. They know not what they do." That day, I made up my mind that I would return to the clinic to pray to God that he would end abortion.

There have been encouraging moments in my time on the sidewalks outside clinics. A couple weeks after my first visit, I was walking back to my car after an hour of sidewalk counseling outside the same abortion clinic when I greeted a young man who was getting out of his car. As I asked him how he was doing, he told me that he was taking his girlfriend to get an abortion. I looked him in the eyes and told him that at the moment of conception all of the baby's genetic information has already been established and that every surgical abortion stops a beating heart. I told him that I was so thankful that his mother chose life for him. Then I asked this young man to pray with me. We prayed, and he gave me his phone number. I then suggested that we walk across the street to the pregnancy care center and allow his girlfriend to get free professional counseling and sonogram services. They did not walk across the street with me to get a free sonogram, but thankfully they chose not to have an abortion that day. I haven't seen that young man again, but I pray that he will never take his girlfriend back to the abortion clinic. In that brief encounter, God provided me encouragement to continue sidewalk counseling.

Within months, I shared many similar conversations with other individuals, many of whom prayed with me. One man, a professing Christian, wept on my shoulder after his girlfriend aborted their baby. As I continued sidewalk counseling in other states, I had the opportunity to talk to several nurses and clinic guards about Jesus. Some were angry with me, while others appreciated my words of hope. I showed my concern for them by asking if I could help them find better employment elsewhere. I remember seeing happiness in the eyes of a young nurse as she exclaimed, "I'm leaving. I quit. Today was my last day working here."

When January 22 came, I flew to Washington, D.C., to meet with the 40 Days for Life leadership team that my friend Carmen had introduced me to, and we all joined the March for Life. I looked across the Washington lawn at a crowd of half a million, made up of a broad spectrum of ages. I thought to myself, *Where have I been?* As an author and a speaker, I had attended large Christian events across the country. I'd also attended professional and college football events. But I had never seen such enthusiasm and conviction from young people as I did at the March for Life.

The day after the march, David Bereit and Shawn Carney spoke at the Hyatt Hotel at Capitol Hill, training 40 Days for Life chapter leaders from all across the world. David stood up and told a story that greatly affected me. In August of 1837, Abraham Lincoln, a twenty-eight-year-old attorney, was invited by a friend to attend an outdoor revival service. Lincoln, several other lawyers, and a couple of doctors jumped in a wagon to trek from Springfield to attend the camp meeting, which was held six miles outside the city. At the camp meeting, Reverend Peter Akers, a gifted communicator, preached a sermon on the dominion of Jesus Christ. His message was to show that God was going to bring a revival in America, but that this spiritual awakening would not come until slavery was eradicated from the country.

Lincoln's biographer G. Frederick Owen recalls how Rev. Akers said, "I believe American slavery will come to an end in some near decade. I think in the sixties." At the climax of his sermon he cried at the top of his voice, "Who can tell but that the man who shall lead us through the strife may be standing in our presence!" Only thirty feet away stood Abraham Lincoln, drinking in his every word.

That night, on the return trip to Springfield, Lincoln was silent. The next morning, when Lincoln arrived late to his office, his partner asked, "What's wrong with you?" Lincoln told him about the sermon and said, "I am utterly unable to shake from myself the conviction that I shall be involved in that tragedy."[3]

Twenty-five years later, Abraham Lincoln was instrumental in making slavery illegal in America by signing the Emancipation Proclamation.

As David Bereit finished telling this story at the Hyatt Hotel in Washington, D.C., he said, "Let me adapt the words of this revivalist and apply them to our generation. Who can tell but that the man or woman who shall lead us through the abolishment of abortion is in our presence today?"

As David spoke those words, my heart pounded. I wanted to be that man, but I was certain that I was no Abraham Lincoln. Yet Lincoln did not abolish slavery by himself. He was assisted by abolitionists such as Frederick Douglass and many, many others. I knew my abilities were limited, but as I listened to David, I also knew that I wanted to play a part in the abolishment of abortion in America in my generation. As an evangelist, I felt a deep conviction that God was truly going to bring an awakening to America, but that we as followers of Jesus Christ needed to repent for our guilt and silence about the shedding of innocent blood. I had a deep conviction that, unlike the Civil War, we could end abortion peacefully through the power of prayer and changed lives.

Frederick Douglass was a former slave from Maryland who became friends with Abraham Lincoln. Douglass wrote in his autobiography about the hypocrisy of professing Christians who both went to church and promoted the evils of slavery in their own community. Douglass wrote,

> I am filled with unutterable loathing when I contemplate the religious pomp and show, together with the horrible inconsistencies, which every where surround me. . . . The slave auctioneer's bell and the church-going bell chime in with each other, and the bitter cries of the heart-broken slave are drowned in the religious shouts of his pious master.[4]

Douglass, Lincoln and other outspoken, genuine Christians were the ones who sought to make slavery illegal in the United States. They were convinced that all people are endowed with the same rights from God: the rights of life, liberty and the pursuit of happiness.

As I have reflected more on Abraham Lincoln, Frederick Douglass, and the abolition of slavery in the United States, I cannot help but see parallels between slavery and the evils done to the preborn in our country today. Not only does my heart cry for true repentance and revival in America, but I am convinced that just one person can make a difference. I also know that the abolition of slavery was a lifetime commitment. Just because slavery became illegal after the signing of the Proclamation did not mean the battle was over. Nevertheless, Lincoln, Douglass and other abolitionists made a difference in their lifetime. Likewise, today one person can shape history by saving just one baby, one mother and one family from abortion.

In this book, you will read stories from counselors, teachers, lawyers, nurses, business leaders, stay-at-home moms, and people from many other professions. We don't all fight against the injustice of abortion in the same way, but we all believe that *one person* can make a difference. We have joined together to write *We Choose Life* because we realize that our society faces a crisis of staggering proportions, similar to that of the injustice of slavery in the early history of our nation.

Abortion is the number one cause of death in the world. To put that into perspective, consider the other leading causes of death around the world. In a single year, approximately half a million people around the world died from breast cancer. According to the World Health Organization, in 2012 alone 1.3 million died from traffic accidents, 1.5 million people died from HIV/AIDS, 3.4 million people died from unclean water, and 7.4 million died from heart disease.[5] But carefully compare those numbers with the following statistic: each year, approximately 42 million babies around the world are killed by intentional abortion. That's over 115,000 babies who are killed each day around the world.[6] 1,290,000 babies will die here in the United States alone. These are not just cold statistics. These are humans—real babies.

On February 3, 1994, Mother Teresa, an elderly woman in her eighties, courageously spoke in front of pro-abortion president Bill Clinton at the National Prayer Breakfast. Mother Teresa said,

> Many people are concerned with the children of India, with the children of Africa where quite a few die of hunger, and so on. Many

people are also concerned about the violence in this great country of the United States. These concerns are very good. But often
these same people are not concerned with the millions being killed
by the deliberate decision of their own mothers. And this is the
greatest destroyer of peace today—abortion which brings people
to such blindness.[7]

Think of it in this manner: What if you found out that thirty-five
kindergarten students were murdered by a maniac two miles from
your home? Wouldn't that anger all of us? And what if you found
out the same thing happened in a hundred cities across America?
Thirty-five hundred children dead. What if it happened the next day,
and then the next? How long would it take us to rise up and say,
"Not in my generation. Let's end the killing"? Yet every day we are
killing just as many Americans in the name of "choice" or women's
"health." How can we stay silent over this issue?

Many people try to ignore what abortion *really is*. Some people
say they are on the fence about abortion and want abortion to be
"safe, legal and rare." Eyewitness testimonies prove that there is *nothing* safe about abortion. For example, former Planned Parenthood
manager Abby Johnson describes her experience when an abortionist asked her to help him hold the ultrasound probe in an ultrasound
suction abortion. Abby recalls her thought process as she initially
tried to justify this first-trimester abortion:

> *The fetus doesn't feel pain.* I had reassured countless women of
> this as I'd been taught by Planned Parenthood. *The fetal tissue
> feels nothing as it is removed. Get a grip, Abby.* This is a simple,
> quick medical procedure. My head was working hard to control
> my responses. . . . The next movement was the sudden jerk of a
> tiny foot as the baby started kicking, as if trying to move away
> from the probing invader. As the cannula pressed in, the baby
> began struggling to turn and twist away. It seemed clear to me
> that the fetus could feel the cannula and did not like the feeling.
> And then the doctor's voice broke though, startling me. "Beam
> me up, Scotty," he said lightheartedly to the nurse. He was telling

her to turn on the suction. . . . I had a sudden urge to yell, "Stop!" To shake the woman and say, "Look at what is happening to your baby! Wake up! Hurry! Stop them!" But even as I thought those words, I looked at my own hand holding the probe. I was one of "them" performing this act.[8]

Dr. Anthony Levatino, who specializes in obstetrics and gynecology, completed 1,200 abortions before becoming pro-life and ceasing to perform abortions. On May 23, 2013, he spoke before members of a congressional committee and described performing a second trimester Dilation and Evacuation (D&E) abortion:

> The toughest part of a D&E abortion is extracting the baby's head. The head of a baby that age is about the size of a large plum and is now free floating inside the uterine cavity. You can be pretty sure you have hold of it if the Sopher clamp is spread about as far as your fingers will allow. You will know you have it right when you crush down on the clamp and see white gelatinous material coming through the cervix. That was the baby's brains. You can then extract the skull pieces. Many times a little face will come out and stare back at you.[9]

Levatino added, "These procedures are brutal by nature."

Abortion is cruel and barbaric, yet Jesus died for individuals who did cruel and barbaric actions towards him. As you read this book, will you please open your heart and mind? Perhaps you could pray, "God, what would you have me to do? Show me your will." You may think, "Who, me? No way! You don't understand what I've done. I've had an abortion." Or, "I've coerced my partner to get an abortion." Or even, "I'm thinking about getting an abortion right now." Well, this book may give you hope. You will read powerful stories of people who faced difficult predicaments. The stories in this book come from people who have been

- unmarried and pregnant at seventeen years of age;
- depressed after learning they were conceived by rape;

- convicted about their job at an abortion clinic, but afraid to give up the much-needed income;
- given an ultrasound that revealed their unborn baby had spina bifida;
- a survivor of a saline-infused abortion.

If you're reading with guilt or a troubled conscience, please know that you are not alone. No matter what you've done—or what has been done to you—God will never abandon you. Regardless of your past, you can be certain that God wants to redeem you, heal you, and use you in a powerful way. A large portion of the New Testament was written by Paul, a murderer and an evil man who experienced a radical life change. Paul wrote to his fellow missionary Timothy,

> This is a trustworthy saying, and everyone should accept it: "Christ Jesus came into the world to save sinners"—and I am the worst of them all. But God had mercy on me so that Christ Jesus could use me as a prime example of his great patience with even the worst sinners. Then others will realize that they, too, can believe in him and receive eternal life. (1 Tim 1:15–16 NLT)

Through God's grace, Paul went from being a violent man—someone who was so blind that he couldn't see the way he was betraying God and hurting others—to being an example of God's love. And Paul wasn't an exception. Christ used Paul's transformation to reveal the most fundamental truth about himself: that he came to save *sinners*.

In the following stories, you will see that the pro-life movement is full of ordinary people who, transformed in their thinking, are now speaking out for the cause of Christ and defending those who cannot speak for themselves. Some of their actions may seem rather simple, but God frequently uses ordinary people to do extraordinary works. The Scripture tells us,

[C]onsider your calling, brothers: not many of you were wise according to worldly standards, not many were powerful, not many were of noble birth. But God chose what is foolish in the world to shame the wise; God chose what is weak in the world to shame the strong; God chose what is low and despised in the world, even things that are not, to bring to nothing things that are, so that no human being might boast in the presence of God. (1 Cor 1:26–29 ESV)

This certainly includes us!

As you read this book, may you be encouraged to let God use you as part of the growing movement of ordinary people who are boldly declaring, "We choose life!"

Dave Sterrett is the founder of Disruptive Truth, a non-profit organization that is disrupting culture with the truth of the gospel. In the last decade, Dave Sterrett has been a spokesman for some of the most innovative Christian organizations that are reaching this generation with the hope of Jesus. He has been invited to speak at many of the nation's colleges and universities, including Yale University, the University of Virginia, and Duke University.

Dave is also the author or co-author of nine books, including the Christian best-seller I Am Second *(Nelson),* Aborting Aristotle *(St. Augustine's Press), and* Is the Bible True . . . Really? *(Moody). You can find more of his writing online at http://www.disruptivetruth.org/.*

1

Why I Left Planned Parenthood

Ramona Treviño

When I look back over the course of my life, I can admit that I've made a lot of mistakes. Some mistakes were made by choice and others by misjudgment. But there's one choice in particular that has and will impact my life forever: the day I chose to accept a position working for Planned Parenthood, the largest abortion provider in the nation. That decision would forever define who I am, and who I want to be for the rest of my life. And little did I know that it would also bring me closer to God.

It was the spring of 2008, our son Elijah had just turned one year old that February, and I was ready to ease my way back into the workplace after taking a year off. I received a call out of the blue from an old friend and former coworker. She was excited to tell me about her new job and to recruit me for an available position at the organization she was now working for.

"Who's it with again?" I asked.

"It's with Planned Parenthood," she said. "But don't worry, they don't do abortions. That's a different and separate affiliation."

Looking back, I often ask myself why I didn't ask more questions at that point. My friend portrayed Planned Parenthood in such a way that I was intrigued by what had her so excited, and I never really took the time to do my research.

Coming from a small town with a population of less than seven hundred, I was largely unfamiliar with Planned Parenthood. My only knowledge of them was that they provided birth control and affordable gynecological care, of sorts. I was naïve and didn't know everything I know today.

Needless to say, I applied for the position. But instead of getting the job as a family planning assistant, I was offered the position of manager on the spot. I was so excited about the opportunity to be manager that I accepted without hesitation. I would run my own "clinic" with my own staff. I would be in a position of power and authority. Not to mention that the job was only three days a week and the pay was decent for a part-time job. What more could one ask for?

I never questioned the clinic's tie to the abortion facility down in the big city. I hoped it would never be an issue. Besides, I was way up in little Sherman, Texas, far away from the atrocities of abortions being performed in Dallas. It didn't apply to me or what I would be doing, right? I pushed any uncomfortable thoughts aside.

But it wasn't long before I got a taste of the reality of working for the abortion giant. The moment came when I did my very first abortion referral counseling. A young woman came in for a pregnancy test. She was a college student and her boyfriend accompanied her. She only wanted to take a pregnancy test and confirm what she already knew to be true. She quickly filled out the required paperwork. In this paperwork, the patient was asked what counseling options she would like if the test was positive. Three choices were given: abortion, adoption, and prenatal. The patient indicated which choice she was considering by placing a check mark next to that option.

As I took the young woman to the back of the clinic to get a urine sample, I showed her boyfriend to one of the examination rooms and asked her to follow me. She supplied me with the sample and then I escorted her to her boyfriend in the exam room. The test only took three minutes and was a definite positive. I gathered all the materials I needed to supply her with prenatal referrals and entered the exam room with the information in hand. But when I confirmed her test results for her with an excited "Congratulations!" she immediately started to cry. Being fairly new in my position, I had failed to look at the "options" section of the paperwork and missed that she had marked "abortion" as her preference.

I was frozen. I wasn't sure exactly what to do at this point. I immediately tried to cover up the look of panic on my face as I stumbled over my words. I began with "I'm sorry . . . abortion is a very difficult decision to make so quickly. Are you sure you don't want to take some time to discuss this with your family?"

She replied, "My family can't know. They would kill me."

I didn't know what to say next. I never received any real training to deal with something like this, and I hardly wanted to advocate for abortion. I wasn't even a licensed counselor. The only experience I had with counseling was nutrition education counseling during my years spent working for the government-sponsored Women, Infants and Children (WIC) program.

This was different. This was a matter of life and death—yet here I was. I found myself in a position of choosing good or evil, right or wrong. Although I knew deep in my heart that I personally didn't believe abortion was right, I had a choice to make. Should I grab my things and quit immediately due to the moral implications of my work? Or should I provide the patient with the referrals and information she requested and wash my hands of whatever decision she made?

I wish I could say I quit and ran out the door. But I didn't. I gave her the referrals she requested and watched her leave just as sad and upset as she was when she arrived. With a heavy heart, I followed her up the hallway and proceeded immediately to my office where I closed the door behind me and cried.

I can't explain exactly why I shed those tears. Maybe it was because I felt the immediate moral implications of what I had just done. Perhaps I was scared of being faced with the same situation again. Either way, I knew I had done something wrong. Yet my mind began to justify my actions. I remember wiping my tears away and saying to myself, "This decision is hers. I'm not here to judge anyone. This is between her and God." As time went on, I found myself praying for the women I counseled at the clinic, even after giving them the telephone number for the abortion facility. It somehow made me feel like I was a better person for doing so, and that God would see that I really did care about these innocent babies and their mothers. Could I have ever been more wrong and twisted?

That was my first taste, my first real taste, of life at Planned Parenthood, and it was followed by more referrals and more rationalizations. The days turned into weeks, and the weeks into months, until next thing I knew I had been there for three years.

Although I was a dedicated manager and employee, I knew I couldn't stay at Planned Parenthood much longer. My love and desire to help people was not a remedy for the tug-of-war I was having with my conscience. It wasn't just the abortion referrals that I struggled with, but the realization that I was never really helping anyone, especially not the women my organization professed to serve.

The promiscuity I observed among teenage girls was enough to turn my stomach. I would counsel girls as young as fourteen and fifteen who would come in for birth control, only to learn that they had already had several sexual partners in their short lifetime. It wasn't the girls themselves and their behavior that bothered me so much, but the idea that Planned Parenthood and its ideology was the solution for such young girls. It no longer made sense simply to distribute contraception to girls and just hope for the best. As a mother, I just could not take it anymore. And as much as I tried, I could not grasp how I was actually helping any of these girls. Was it by giving them birth control, or by cleaning up their STDs? Something had to change.

Something did change in December 2010. I changed the station. The radio station, that is. One evening after work, I went to the local Walmart to pick up a few last-minute Christmas gifts. I sat in my car and started flipping through the AM radio stations. I cannot say why on earth I was flipping through the AM stations, but—as the Holy Spirit would have it—that's what I did. Something caught my ear and I abruptly stopped on 910 AM. The topic for the night was pro-life questions and answers. Women called in to the show to discuss their abortion experiences with Planned Parenthood. All of a sudden, my ears were like antennas. I was tuned in to each and every word, and my mind raced a million miles per second.

So many callers shared their sad stories. Each woman told a different story, but the one common factor was always Planned Parenthood. Planned Parenthood had destroyed their lives. The same Planned Parenthood that I represented, the Planned Parenthood that I used to defend. I was guilty of something, but what? That was the question I had been searching for answers to. As I continued listening to the radio program, the truth began to present itself. The truth about Planned Parenthood, the abortion industry, and abortifacient contraceptives triggered something deep within me.

That night I couldn't sleep. There were so many emotions, thoughts and questions left unanswered. Even so, I suppressed my feelings and continued with my work. Christmas was just around the corner and I didn't want any of these new revelations to interfere with holiday preparations. Besides, I would soon have some days off which would allow me to avoid work altogether. It wasn't until after the New Year that I would revisit the new revelations that had begun to undermine my assumptions about my work at the clinic.

I continued to work as usual, but now I tuned in to Catholic radio on my way to and from the "clinic." With every trip, I learned something new about life issues and the pro-life battle. It seemed as though the Holy Spirit knew just when I would be tuning in—at just the right time—to have more of my questions answered. It was during my thirty-minute commute to work that I heard of Abby Johnson for the first time.

I didn't catch the whole interview with Abby. I only heard the end of her interview, but I had a chance to hear about her book, *Unplanned,* and that she was a former Planned Parenthood director who had a conversion and got out. My immediate thought was that I had to get my hands on this book. Maybe this book would be the missing puzzle piece I had been searching for. But I soon suppressed the idea and decided not to purchase Abby's book.

More time passed and I still didn't know what to do. I began emailing my résumé out to different job listings in hopes that someone would offer me an interview. I was unsuccessful. January passed and I began to grow weary because I still had no idea what I was going to do. In my heart, I knew I was no longer able to justify the abortion referrals, nor could I ignore the connection abortion had with contraceptives. I needed to do something soon, but I was getting nowhere in the new job search.

Without another job lined up, there was no way I could quit my current job. What would we do without my income? How would we pay the mortgage and all our other bills? How could we afford to put food on the table and take care of our children? My husband couldn't bear all of the financial responsibilities by himself. We were not prepared to live on only one income. My lack of preparation and financial planning left me feeling helpless and hopeless. I had nowhere to turn if I left Planned Parenthood.

But God had other plans for me. He would not abandon me. I didn't have to feel helpless and hopeless. There was no reason to feel lost and afraid. God was in control, and I just needed to have faith . . . but I wasn't quite ready for that yet. My walk with Christ had grown cold and distant during the time I worked for Planned Parenthood. Because of my work, I found myself sitting in the pews guilt-ridden . . . on the days when we did attend. Where previously we attended church every Sunday, we now attended only infrequently. I found myself sitting there battling with my conscience, asking myself if there even was a God and, if so, whether He would really be angry with me for where I worked. But I was now at the point where I wanted my relationship with Christ back. I wanted to reconcile with my Creator.

It was March and the season of Lent was fast approaching. Being a Catholic Christian, I felt this would be the perfect time to ask for God's grace and forgiveness. This was a time of reflection and meditation, a time for forgiveness and resurrection. This year Lent meant so much more than the usual sacrifice of fast food and sodas. I chose to do something with more meaning, something that would help me focus more on Christ. I decided not only to read and meditate on Scripture daily, but to also pray the holy rosary every evening before bedtime, focusing on the life of Christ, all while still working for Planned Parenthood.

While I was focusing on prayer and devotion, something else was happening simultaneously outside the Planned Parenthood in Sherman. Sherman's very first 40 Days for Life campaign was going on right in front of the facility I worked at. A few days into the campaign, everyone on my staff was gone and I had just finished with my end-of-the-day duties. As I headed for my car, I looked up and noticed a sweet lady across the parking lot give me a smile, a nod, and an apprehensive wave. She was a prayer warrior, but my colleagues and I considered her a "protestor." I smiled, waved back, and hurried to get into my car as fast as possible. I was experiencing a wide range of emotions as I left. One in particular was a feeling of disappointment: I had promised myself that I would reach out to someone in the 40 Days for Life campaign when I had the chance. I chickened out. I thought to myself, *Maybe next time.*

Next time came sooner than I thought it would. I had barely started down the street when I realized that I had forgotten the deposit. Since it was a Friday, I couldn't just leave it for tomorrow, because I wouldn't be back again until Tuesday. So I went back. I ran inside, grabbed the deposit bag, and hurried back to my car. But this time something was different. I could feel the eyes of the sweet woman across the way staring at me. I had a second chance. I heard the faint voice of someone say to me, *Go.* I felt as though I had been shoved gently from behind and told again, *Go to her.* I dropped the deposit bag in the car, took a deep breath, and proceeded to where the woman was standing.

There was definitely a feeling of apprehension as I walked toward her. I wonder what she was thinking as she watched me approach. I was nervous, afraid of what she might say or think of me. I can't remember all of the details of our conversation, but I remember telling her who I was and why I wanted to leave Planned Parenthood. We had a good conversation that ended in prayer. She gave me a hug, and I thanked her. As I turned to head back to my car, a man approached me. He was a very tall, bearded man wearing a pro-life T-shirt. He introduced himself, and I shared my story again. He asked if I had heard of Abby Johnson. It was so obvious that God wanted me to read her story because, as God would have it, this man just happened to have a copy of Abby's book, *Unplanned,* in his truck.

The gentlemen and I parted ways, and he promised to lift me up in prayer as well as to circulate my résumé around to trusted friends. I went home that night filled with hope and immediately began reading Abby's book. I was so engrossed in the story that I couldn't put it down. The story of Abby's courage to leave the abortion industry was more than inspirational—it was exactly what I needed to know so that I might be able to do the same.

The 40 Days for Life campaign continued outside my clinic and with every passing day I felt the loving support from the prayers of the faithful who participated. Although my job search was not successful, their prayers gave me the hope and strength to hold on to my faith. But I was growing weary. How much longer would I have to endure life at Planned Parenthood? How many more abortion referrals would I be able to escape from? I needed to make a decision once for all. Do I leave without a job? What if I don't find another job? Will God ever forgive me? Will I ever be able to forgive myself? I was bombarded by questions that seemed to have no answers.

As Lent concluded, the 40 Days for Life team wrapped up their prayers, sacrifice, and peaceful vigil, and I wrapped up my forty days of reading Scripture and praying the rosary. Just a few days later I received a call from a woman named Lauren Muzyka. (Lauren's story appears in Chapter 6.) Lauren was one of the members of the 40 Days for Life national team and worked as their campaign strategist. She called and left a sweet message sharing her desire to help me. I eagerly called her back.

Most of the conversation was a blur, but I remember pouring my heart out to this perfect stranger. I trusted her, and I knew she really wanted to help me. At this point, I knew I wanted to leave my position with Planned Parenthood, but I still didn't know what to do without a job lined up. Lauren understood my dilemma, and she lifted me up in prayer. As the days passed, we kept in touch and I shared with her all of my worries, doubts, and concerns. Again, she prayed for me and helped me to sort through all I had experienced during my years at Planned Parenthood.

God knew it would take more than just prayers and uplifting phone calls for me to take what felt like a leap into the unknown. I needed to take a huge leap of faith in order to cut ties with the number one abortion provider in the country, and God knew it wouldn't be easy. Although I had been preparing myself spiritually, and I had begun to understand my own culpability for my association with abortion, something was still missing.

That missing piece came on Sunday morning, May 1, 2011. My family and I had been attending church regularly since the beginning of Lent and this Sunday wasn't any different. Except that this Sunday was Divine Mercy Sunday. Divine Mercy, simply put, is a feast day in which we receive abundant graces, Jesus's forgiveness and mercy. The message is one of hope and trust in our Lord and Savior Jesus Christ. That morning I sat in the pews asking God to guide me and help me to find a way out of Planned Parenthood. A flood of tears streamed down my face as I sat there asking for God's forgiveness for what I had done with my life. I began to feel a peace come over me. I sensed God say to me, "Trust in me. I forgive you. Leave everything behind and follow me."

This was what that I had been waiting for. I needed to hear the voice of God. I left church knowing exactly what needed to be done.

That Monday afternoon, I called Lauren. I was excited to tell her that I would be leaving at the end of the month—with or without a job! But when I woke up on Tuesday morning, I sensed the Holy Spirit speaking to me again, "What are you waiting for? Trust in me."

I knew what I had to do. Again I called Lauren excited with the news that my last day would be that Friday, May 6, instead of at the end of the month as previously discussed. She was equally excited and guided me about what to do next. When Friday evening rolled around and everyone had left, I left behind my letter of resignation, the clinic keys, and my former self. I walked out the door and never looked back.

I had done it! I had taken the giant leap of faith that Christ was calling me to take. Not only did I leap into his loving and merciful arms, but I found out what it means to have faith. There was no other job waiting for me when I left Planned Parenthood. There was of course my last paycheck, some 401(k) money, and some much-appreciated donations from some wonderful, loving Christians. But that didn't last forever, nor did I expect it to. Yet by the grace of God we continued to make ends meet.

Not only did I find work within a month after leaving Planned Parenthood, but I found myself expecting a baby as well. God blessed us with a new little boy who was born in March of 2012.

Today I look back, a little over a year after leaving Planned Parenthood, and I know without a shadow of a doubt that I did the right thing. Yes, my family and I have struggled financially. Yet every hurdle, every struggle, every worry has been more than worth it. You see, just three short months after I left my post as Sherman's clinic manager, that location was closed down for good!

Many people have asked if my quitting had anything to do with the clinic closing. Many have asked if it was because of the 40 Days for Life vigil held there that year. I don't have answers to their questions. But this I do know: in the spring of 2011 many people said "yes" to God and "yes" to whatever he was asking of them. And that spring we all witnessed miracles all around. The faithful who showed up to pray witnessed a woman converted and a Planned Parenthood clinic closed forever, and I witnessed what God looks like in the faces of all of those who prayed for me and loved me. They loved me, a stranger, a fool, a sinner.

I know that people wonder if there is a God. They wonder where he is and why bad things happen. But if you ever doubt for even one second, just remember my story and know that God reveals himself through our conscience. All we have to do is listen and take a step of faith towards Christ.

Today I find myself answering God's call. I am currently a public speaker, sharing my testimony about what I experienced while working at Planned Parenthood with pro-life groups around the country. The pro-life battle is one that must be won, and I couldn't be happier to call myself one of God's soldiers in this fight. I will not fear. For once one knows the truth that life begins at conception, one must defend the truth. It's that simple.

2

How I Finally Chose Life

Jewels Green

I found out I was pregnant for the first time just three weeks before Christmas. The news didn't feel like unwrapping an early present, though. It felt more like that nearly indescribable sensation I'd gotten in the pit of my stomach when I was nine years old and I found where my mother had hidden my wrapped gifts. I had carefully, soundlessly, and very slowly unwrapped just the one end of the large rectangular box wrapped in shiny red paper. And there it was. I had wanted that Tri-Lab-Pak children's microscope and science experiment set so badly I'd dreamed about it. But I'd broken the rules only to find out I'd be getting exactly what I wanted, and that it was too soon for it to be mine.

When I discovered I was unexpectedly pregnant at seventeen—an unmarried, drug-abusing high school dropout—I did not consider abortion as an alternative. In fact, I already thought of myself as a new mother. I actually stopped using drugs, went to the library and checked out a book titled *Under 18 and Pregnant,* and started to read it to prepare for parenthood. I scheduled my first prenatal check-up. I called the local public assistance office to learn how to apply for medical assistance. I was getting ready to raise my child.

Then the pressure began from all sides—everyone I loved and trusted in my life wanted me to have an abortion. It was suffocating and relentless. I felt alone. I felt trapped. I felt abandoned.

The first number I called in the phone book wasn't an abortion clinic at all, but just a recording that began with the words, "By the time you miss your second period, your baby's heart has begun to beat." Then I heard the little but rapid *foom-foom-foom-foom-foom* of a recorded fetal heartbeat. The voice went on to describe the horror of abortion, and explained in terrifying detail the story of a mother of two who was rushed to a hospital after a legal abortion at a local clinic and then bled to death. I refused to consider such an outcome. I was terrified. But my heart grew cold. My resolve crumbled.

I let my boyfriend take me to the abortion clinic. After blood work and counseling and paying, it came time to disrobe for surgery. I literally *ran* out of the office in the hope of saving my baby. My rescue attempt failed when two days later, at nine and a half weeks' gestation, I had the abortion. It nearly killed me; not the surgical procedure, but the psychological aftermath. I called that well-intentioned pro-life recording again and again and again in the days following my abortion. The recorded heartbeat became my inner torturous mantra and I heard it everywhere: *foom-foom-foom-foom-foom* . . . STOP.

Just a few weeks after my abortion I attempted suicide and ended up in an adolescent psychiatric ward for a month to recover. The mind is a dark and slippery place, full of unexpected twists, and it is all too easy to lose footing and tumble into a crevasse where a troubled soul can become trapped.

Within just a few months of my own traumatic abortion experience and weeks after my discharge from the psych unit, I found myself on a local pro-choice sponsored bus trip to Washington, D.C., to march in support of abortion rights. Soon after the march I began volunteering as an escort for a first-trimester abortion clinic (not the clinic where I had my abortion).

Blindly latching onto the position that was opposed to my innermost heart shielded me from further inner turmoil. I was trying to convince myself that abortion wasn't wrong. When I applied for a job at the abortion clinic where I volunteered, I wrote an essay about why I thought I'd make a good abortion clinic worker. I shared my own personal experience with abortion (minus the ambivalence, coercion, and subsequent emotional maelstrom) as well as my zeal for the right to abortion (I marched on Washington!) and why I thought this combination made me the ideal candidate for an entry-level position at the abortion clinic. It worked. I was hired.

I completely bought the bill of goods I was sold: that abortion was somehow linked to women's equality; that giving birth and making an adoption plan for an unwanted or ill-timed child (rather than killing it) was somehow unduly burdensome for a pregnant mother; and that countless women would die if abortion were illegal. Combine all of this with my unconscious but overwhelming need to repress/forget/ignore/transform my personal feelings about *my* abortion—and my longing for *my* lost child—and it created the perfect recipe for a die-hard, closed-minded, abortion rights advocate.

In my five years working at the abortion clinic I learned every job except doctor and nurse. I even came in early to sweep up cigarette butts on the ground outside the doors and spent one Sunday painting the stalls in the staff bathroom. My framed calligraphy adorned the waiting room wall ("Register to Vote! Elect Pro-Choice Legislators!"). I eagerly accepted new challenges, but by far the hardest job I learned was that of autoclave technician. An autoclave looks like an oversized microwave and it's used to sterilize surgical instruments. The autoclave technician is essentially a glorified dishwasher. A dishwasher for bloody metal instruments.

The other function of the autoclave room was to provide a place where the parts of the aborted child could be counted and reassembled to ensure a complete abortion. If any body parts were left inside the uterus, it could lead to infection. The jars that were attached to the

suction machines were disconnected after each abortion and passed
through little windows in the walls to the autoclave technician.

Working in the autoclave room was never, ever, easy. I saw my
lost child in every transparent glass jar of aborted baby parts. I
started having nightmares that were no longer only about my lost
baby—whom I thought about often and cried about and missed—
but of all of the babies killed by abortion where I worked every
day, all of the babies killed by abortion everywhere. My sleep was
haunted by tiny limbless phantom babies. But even then, my desire
to survive in a world without my child—because I'd killed him—
warped my mind into believing that if all of these strong, capable
women I worked with thought abortion was guiltlessly permissible,
I must be able to believe that, too.

One night after working the autoclave my nightmares about
dead babies were so gruesome and terrifying and intense that I
decided to meet with the clinic's director to talk about my feelings. She was very understanding, honest, and painfully forthright
when she told me, "What we do here is end a life. Pure and simple.
There is no disputing this fact. You need to be OK with this to work
here." So I pushed down the unpleasantness, muzzled my pesky
conscience, and after a few days I decided I was OK with what we
did there—end a life—and God help me, I went back. And I kept
going back, day after day, year after year.

On a cold day not so long ago, I found myself contemplating
the bizarre and unnatural process of in-vitro fertilization and surrogacy. An acquaintance of mine agreed to be a surrogate mother
for a friend of hers and shared with me the details of the process.
I slowly began questioning the rightness of creating life in a labo-
ratory. My friend had joined a support group for surrogates and
told me of a mother whose contract included genetic testing on
the baby she was carrying for an infertile couple. When the results
indicated the child would be born with Down syndrome, she was
offered payment of her surrogacy contract in full to abort—and

she did. That was it. This was my "aha moment," when my mental attitude shifted completely and I finally (finally!) understood: abortion kills an innocent human being . . . every time. Pregnancy was now a commercial transaction: the tiny, helpless, growing human baby a commodity to be created, sold, bought, and disposed of at will—how gruesome and reprehensible—and I had been a part of that barbaric "industry" for years. I cried. I prayed. I was now pro-life. My entire worldview shifted 180 degrees.

Within weeks of self-identifying as pro-life I began donating my time, talents, and treasure to the cause. I joined several national and local pro-life groups and sought out my local chapter of 40 Days for Life. My first prayer vigil was outside of the hospital where my third son was born, and where abortions are performed. We walked and prayed and I sang one of my favorite hymns from childhood. It was this—the peaceful, prayerful presence of dedicated individuals offering hope, support, and real resources for pregnant mothers considering abortion—that convinced me I'd made the right choice by changing my mind on abortion.

Sharing my story with others has been the most difficult, yet most transformative, thing I have ever done. I hope and pray that those who hear the painful, shameful details of my past will come to embrace the truth that conversion is real—and entirely possible. That a peaceful, prayerful presence at the abortion clinics has to include compassionate outreach, practical resources, and support for the pregnant mother, and prayers for conversion of the workers inside. They are not the enemy, they are not all evil—abortion is the enemy, abortion is evil.

3

How a Liberal Atheist Professor Changed His Mind

Mike Adams

On the evening of April 30, 2009, Dr. Mike Adams arrived on the campus of the University of Massachusetts at Amherst. He was scheduled to give a talk on abortion from the pro-life perspective. As he was escorted to the hall where the speech was to take place, he saw a giant sign posted on the wall of the building. Across the banner, these three words were emblazoned: "F*** MIKE ADAMS."

After getting a good laugh from the banner, Dr. Adams headed inside the building, where he saw a couple dozen protestors holding signs. He approached them and asked why they had posted such a vile sign as a greeting to a guest. The protestors identified themselves as members of the Amherst Socialist Party. Next, they dropped a bomb on him, saying, "We didn't make the sign. It was the UMass Coalition against Hate." You can't make this stuff up. It's positively Orwellian!

Later that night, two of the protestors were arrested for standing up and screaming profanities during Dr. Adams's speech. The former pro-choice atheist turned pro-life apologist could only shake his head and laugh. Sixteen years earlier, he had been one of them.

—Dave Sterrett

In the summer of 1993, I went home for my ten-year high school reunion. I was so excited I could hardly sleep all week. The kid who finished 734th in a class of 740 had made quite a turn-around. Over a span of ten years, I had gone off to junior college and earned an associate's degree in psychology. Next, I added a bachelor's degree in psychology. Then, I earned a master's in social psychology. Finally, I topped it off with a doctorate in criminology. I could hardly wait to see my old classmates and tell them that I had just been hired as a college professor. I could not wait to see their reaction as I told them that the guy who failed English four times in high school was now a published author. But those were not the only changes that had taken place over the course of ten years. I had also become an atheist and a strong proponent of abortion rights.

With all that education, I should have known better. When my professors told me the object of abortion was "nothing more than a clump of cells," I should have known that there was a powerful incentive for me to believe them. I should have known there was a psychological motive to avoid examining all of the evidence in the debate. If psychology had taught me anything, it was that attitudes and beliefs do not always drive our behavior. Often, it is our behavior that drives our attitudes and beliefs.

My behavior in those days was reprehensible. But it did not become that way overnight. It was all part of a gradual decline that began during my senior year in high school. A torn Achilles tendon ended my dreams of becoming a professional soccer player. And that's when I started to smoke and drink heavily and run around with women whose affections assuaged my damaged self-esteem.

By the end of my first semester in junior college, I called myself an agnostic. And that helped accelerate the decline in my quality of life. As an undergraduate, I gradually increased my consumption of alcohol and my casual relationships with women. In 1989, I joined a musical duo, which turned into a full-time job. As a traveling musician, I further increased my consumption of alcohol. I not only abused alcohol but also badly used the women I met at the bars where I played. It is true that many women who follow musicians are looking for the same thing. But that isn't true of all of them. I usually kept a steady girlfriend as well as a couple of extra women on the side. And because I did not behave responsibly with them, I needed a backup plan. That's how I came to convince myself that abortion was permissible. My beliefs about abortion had nothing to do with moral reasoning. It was all about rationalizing a lifestyle. It was about finding a way, psychologically speaking, of dealing with unpleasant thoughts about the risks I was taking.

I'm convinced that there are others like me—they begin studying psychology because of a desire to solve their own problems, not because they want to help other people. I learned about a lot of theories as a student of psychology. But I always seemed to lack the objectivity necessary to apply them to my own conduct.

Cognitive dissonance is a psychological theory that asserts that human beings desire consistency in their cognitive life. In other words, it teaches that our beliefs and values and awareness of our behavior must all mesh with one another. When we feel tension (dissonance) between inconsistent beliefs and values, we sometimes adopt a new belief in an attempt to resolve the tension and achieve consonance (the opposite of dissonance). As a student of psychology, I provided a living example of that theory without even realizing it.

Because I was reasonably intelligent, I knew that sleeping with numerous women created a real risk of an unplanned pregnancy. I also knew that as a musician and student I was in no position to raise a child. But I was also raised to believe that abortion was wrong. So I experienced real tension (cognitive dissonance) between my values and the awareness of my risky behavior and the consequences it might bring. So I took the easy way out: I adopted the bland assertions of pro-choice advocates who claimed that the preborn were not human.

And so my behavior drove my attitudes. That is how the vicious cycle began. Once I had convinced myself that abortion was permissible because the preborn were not human, I sought out women who believed the same thing. In the fall of 1990, I went to the extreme of actually breaking up with a girlfriend as soon as she told me she would never have an abortion. Over the course of the next several years, I only dated women who were pro-choice. In other words, I would only date a woman if she was committed to giving me sex without the prospect of parenthood.

But all that changed in 1993 when I came home for that ten-year high school reunion. By God's divine providence, there were a couple of guests staying at my parents' house in Houston. Their names were Steve and Lisa Chambers. They were old friends whom we had first met in 1969 when my mother was doing visitation for Clear Lake Baptist Church. That old church was just about a mile away from Clear Lake High School—the school from which I would barely graduate 14 years later. After I became an atheist and a liberal, Lisa Chambers refused to give up on me. Every time she saw me, she would try to plant a stone in my shoe in the hope that I would re-think at least one of my political or religious positions.

In 1993, when I sat down to eat breakfast with her at my parents' house, she decided to whittle away at my pro-choice position. After I admitted that I was pro-choice, she began telling me about a friend of one of her sons who had worked at a crisis pregnancy center, or CPC. That was when I first heard about the effects that ultrasound technology was having on a woman's likelihood of going through with an abortion.

After telling me a little bit about ultrasound technology, Lisa talked about a man named Bernard Nathanson who was the co-founder of the National Abortion Rights Action League, or NARAL. She explained that Dr. Nathanson had performed hundreds of abortions, including one on his girlfriend. But after aborting his own child, Dr. Nathanson eventually saw an ultrasound of an actual abortion procedure. It changed his life forever.

Bernard Nathanson would later convert to Roman Catholicism and join the pro-life movement. He also made a film called *The Silent Scream*, which featured an ultrasound of an actual abortion as it was taking place. Lisa Chambers had seen the film and she recommended that I watch it, too. She also took the time to describe to me the ultrasound image of the child as it attempted to escape from the medical instrument that was methodically dismembering it. She described the image of the baby's mouth opening and trying to scream—although no one could hear it from within the mother's womb. Lisa spent no more than a few minutes describing that imagery, but I could not seem to get it out of my mind.

So I eventually watched *The Silent Scream*, and I also listened to what critics said about the movie. I was unimpressed with virtually all of what the critics had to say. The only rebuttal I ever heard in response to the movie's central claim—that the preborn actually felt the pain of abortion—was the so-called "reflex" argument. This was simply the claim that the baby was not recoiling in pain as a result of being dismembered by the surgeon's knife. Instead, it was argued that the baby was merely reacting reflexively to being touched by an unknown object. But this argument fails for one simple reason: if it has fully functioning reflexes, then the baby is a living being. It is not a mere blob of tissue.

Whether it was actively fighting or reflexively reacting, the thing I saw was surely living. And if it was a living being, then how could one escape the conclusion that it was a living human being? Surely no one could assert that it was a member of another species until its birth.

The criminologist in me also had questions concerning the presumed innocence of the unborn child: If there is any ambiguity about whether the preborn is human, then should it not be resolved in favor of calling it a human being? In the eyes of the law, is it not better to let ten guilty men go free than wrongfully to punish one innocent man? And if the preborn human being has never committed a crime, then doesn't abortion always kill an innocent human being without due process?

While some have argued that the constitution includes an "implicit right to privacy," I saw nothing of the sort actually written into the United States Constitution. Instead, I saw specific mention of the "person," who is entitled to both "due process" and "equal protection." The words are there and need not be read into a "living" constitution—ironically, in order to justify killing.

Eventually, I concluded that it is up to the proponents of abortion to justify their distinction between an innocent human being and a "person." The burden of proof rests upon those who wish to sentence the preborn to death. They must show that "it" is not a person. For years, I've been asking pro-abortion advocates to draw that distinction and I've never been satisfied with their answers. Few have even tried to supply an answer based on science and reason. Ironically, since becoming a Christian I have found that I do not need to rely on religion to make the case for life. Science and reason are enough. Of course, like life itself, both are gifts from a God who is at once a lover of life and the author of truth.

When one examines my journey from abortion-choice advocate to pro-life activist, there is obvious cause for alarm. How could a man spend ten years in college, earn an MS in psychology and a PhD in criminology, and never even think about the central question in the abortion debate? The fact that people were calling me "Dr." before I ever seriously answered the question "Are the preborn human?" is disturbing. It speaks volumes about the lack of intellectual diversity in higher education.

However, there is also good news to be drawn from an examination of my conversion on the issue of abortion. Notice that it all began with one person deciding to plant a stone in my shoe. Lisa Chambers did not set out to argue with me until I changed my mind.

She simply spent about fifteen minutes with me and made sure that I began to think seriously about the central question in the abortion debate: are the preborn living human beings? As I write the closing words of this brief chapter, I am 2,000 miles from home. In three hours, I will speak to two hundred students here in Colorado. We'll talk about how to defend life using logic paired with basic scientific evidence. I'll fly to Pennsylvania in a few weeks to do the same thing. I am scheduled to travel to North Carolina a few weeks later to give that message again. After nineteen years, the stone Lisa Chambers planted in my shoe is still there. As I travel around the country, I still feel its presence with every step I take. It helps keep me focused on the central issue in this debate over life and death.

My friend and pro-life attorney David French often says, "You only get flak when you're flying over the target." That is why protestors do not offend me. In fact, they inspire me.

4

Redeemed

Jon Lineberger

In the spring of my junior year in high school my girlfriend got pregnant. We were both only seventeen years old. Initially, I was in disbelief. Then I experienced a range of emotions, feeling closer to my girlfriend and scared at the same time. To make matters worse, I was a selfish, immature, co-dependent, and controlling boyfriend in an unfaithful, emotionally abusive, and dysfunctional relationship. As the reality of the pregnancy sank in I began to feel overwhelmed, and then spiraled into anxiety and panic. What were we going to do?

This can't happen, I thought. My father was the pastor of a church in town. I knew how cruel and judgmental people can sometimes be and I wondered what people in our community would think and say when they found out. I thought that if the members of my father's church found out that the pastor's son got his girlfriend pregnant, my father would lose his job. I had already brought so much shame on my family and I didn't want to contribute any more. Even if my father wasn't asked to step down from being pastor of the church, I thought he would quit anyway because he would be too embarrassed to stand in front of people every Sunday and lead them when his own son was out of control.

I began to think over all of my options. I felt so trapped that I even contemplated suicide and thought through different ways to get the job done. I didn't want to have to face the consequences of my actions. I already didn't like my life. I was a terrible student in school, had low self-esteem, and I'd made so many bad, impulsive decisions. I constantly dwelt on those bad decisions and the hurt I had experienced—so much that I hated my life and wished I had never been born. I didn't think I would ever be able to get out of the mess I had made. And now more than ever I didn't want to own up to my careless decisions. I was still just a kid, but I was doing adult things and now, suddenly, I was forced to grapple with adult consequences.

If only I had listened to my parents and obeyed them, I wouldn't have been in this situation, but I wanted to do what I wanted to do. I was selfish and chased after pleasure for myself. I didn't think through how my actions could hurt other people, especially those who loved me. I impulsively acted on whatever fun thought came to mind. Honestly, I never considered consequences, because I wanted immediate satisfaction. Having ADHD didn't help. I wanted what I wanted when I wanted it—at least, that's what I thought. Until then, I had brushed off my parents' warnings by telling myself, "That could never happen to me." I wish I had heeded the instruction that sex is a gift from God that comes with responsibilities—a gift that, if practiced outside of God's boundaries, incurs painful consequences. Indulging in activities outside of God's design and parameters may be fun for a while, but in the end there will always be consequences.

After weeks, even months, of agonizing over what to do, we secretly decided on an abortion. I knew that abortion was wrong and a sin, but I was desperate. I just wanted the situation to be over. I needed a "quick fix" to get myself out of the mess I was in. Like King David, I was looking for a way to cover up and hide my sin, and I tried to do so by committing another sin (2 Sam 11). But two wrongs don't make a right. Once you start down the path of sin it's not an easy road to get off. Sin begets sin. I still wasn't thinking about the future consequences of my actions. I was desperate for an immediate solution and didn't count the cost, just as I hadn't counted the cost of having sex before I was married. I was much too immature to handle that kind of responsibility or to understand the lasting effects of my decisions. After determining what we would do, we waited several months until school was out for the summer to follow through with the abortion.

Thinking back, I don't remember a lot because I tried to block much of it out. I do remember pulling into the parking lot and walking inside the abortion clinic. It was a terrible sensation. The place had a cold and sterile feeling. It felt as though God was absent from that place. Everyone in the waiting room had their heads down and no one looked anyone else in the eyes. I tried to numb myself by putting the purpose of our visit out of my mind and trying to think of it as just a doctor visit. Because my girlfriend's pregnancy was so far advanced, the abortion was a two-day procedure. I remember that during the first day they broke her water and the reality of what we were doing suddenly sank in. Regret and panic came over me and I asked the doctor, "Can we stop it? Can we go back now? Can we have the child?" My girlfriend shook her head no. That was when the guilt and acknowledgement of the sin we were committing became real to me. She also told me that the child we were aborting was a boy. My stomach knotted.

After the abortion, I tried to disassociate myself from the event and block it out of my mind, but the guilt and depression I began to feel only grew increasingly worse. I began to drink more as a way to self-medicate and escape reality, and I acted more recklessly than before.

My senior year things got a lot worse. I found myself continuing to get in more and more trouble and even spent a weekend in jail. I was kicked off the football team just a few games into the season. My life continued to spiral out of control and I felt hopeless. I sank deeper and deeper into depression as I contemplated the mess I had made of my life.

Those around me who cared for me and loved me realized that I was at a dangerous place in life. A month into my senior year I had an in-school suspension for getting into a fight when I was called into the assistant principal's office. When I arrived, my parents were sitting in front of his desk. The assistant principal told me that I was out of control and that I could no longer stay at the school, but he promised to allow me to walk with the rest of my class at graduation if I attended rehab. My parents were concerned and worried for me. They could see how depressed I had become. I was self-medicating my mental anguish with alcohol to escape from reality. I was so ashamed of my life I couldn't even look people in the eyes.

Rehab was good for me in the sense that it got me out of a dangerous place in life, but I still did not yet turn my life over to the Lord. I continued to make bad decisions and hang around other people who weren't living their lives for the Lord. The old saying is true: you do become like the people you hang out with. I'm not blaming others for my actions, but I also couldn't escape the truth found in Scripture: "Do not be misled: 'Bad company corrupts good character'" (1 Cor 15:33).

After another year and a half of living for myself, I cried out to Jesus to give me another chance at life. By the grace of God and the faithful prayers of my parents, I eventually made a decision to live my life for Christ. Just the way the father ran to meet the prodigal son, Jesus welcomed me home with open arms. He forgave me and began to work in my life to right the wrongs I had done. I felt like I could finally breathe. Like I had been at the bottom of a dog pile and someone had come in and started pulling people off me. I knew it was the Lord peeling away all the layers of sin and guilt and shame that I had spent years covering my life with. That was the greatest day of my life and a huge turning point for me.

Still, deciding to live for Christ didn't mean that all of my pain and guilt immediately went away. Because of God's love, grace, and mercy, I've been able to stop punishing myself for my past sins, but it has taken time and prayer to get to this point. I know God has forgiven me of my sins, and yet I still feel great remorse for the abortion I was a part of. Even though I have been forgiven, there are still scars that I will bear. For a long time, I felt like there were consequences I would still have to face for the sins I'd committed in the past.

Before I got married, I felt like I needed to tell my future wife about my past. I think most people assume when they are just starting out that they will be able to have a fulfilling family life. Because of my past, I had a different perspective. I thought that God might not bless me with children because of what I had done. I knew I certainly did not deserve to have children. And even if God did give us children, I felt he would never bless us with a boy. I needed my future wife to know this because I did not want her to unknowingly pay consequences for my previous decisions. But she was a true example of God's love, grace and mercy—she forgave me for my past and married me anyway.

A few years after we married, my wife became pregnant. I was overjoyed, but I still held my breath, hesitating to get too excited and wondering if God would truly bless us with a child. I knew I didn't deserve any children at all and I felt that if there were complications in the pregnancy, the birth, or even in the child itself, it would be my fault. In the back of my mind I worried that my sin of abortion would bring negative consequences onto our child. I kept these feelings secret, but they were always present. I prayed night after night on my knees that my sins would not be passed on to our child. Other times I would pray with my hand on my wife's belly that God would protect our child and give us a happy healthy baby.

I felt unworthy to have a healthy child and prepared myself for whatever would come. The time finally came to go in for a sonogram.

When the nurse told us that the baby was a girl, and that she looked healthy, I was so thankful. The day our first daughter arrived was one of the best days of my life. She was a beautiful healthy baby. I could not believe that God had blessed us with this child. Every night I would get on my knees beside her crib and thank God for her. I would pray to God that my sins would not be passed on to my children.

Eleven months later my wife was pregnant again. I was so happy. I didn't deserve any child and God had already blessed me with a wonderful, beautiful daughter. Again, I prayed for and over this baby the same prayers I prayed for the first. The day came for us to get a sonogram. As we entered the doctor's office, I held my wife's hand praying again for a healthy happy child. When the sonographer said it was another girl and that she was healthy I was so grateful that God would bless me with another healthy girl. I didn't deserve one healthy child, let alone two. She was born perfect just like our first daughter. These two girls became two of the greatest joys in my life, and I continued to pray that my sins would not be passed on to future generations of my family.

A little over two years later we discovered that my wife was pregnant for a third time. We again prayed for the Lord to give us a happy and healthy child. As I prayed for the baby, I thought to myself, "God has been so good to me, better than I deserve, but would God bless me with a son?" Many times I prayed, "God you've given me more than I deserve and I am unworthy to ask you for more. I am so grateful for the two beautiful girls you've given me. Lord, please bless me with a son, but most of all a healthy baby."

When the day finally came for the sonogram, I was so nervous. I told God that I would be grateful for whatever he blessed us with, but that I would love to have a son. It is difficult to describe, but I still felt in a way that the punishment I would pay for my sin was that I would not have a son. As we entered our private room at the doctor's office the anticipation intensified. Then the nurse told us, "It's a boy!" At that moment I couldn't contain my emotions. Tears of happiness burst into my eyes and I laughed out loud with joy just the way I did for our first two girls. In that instant I felt and experienced the full and complete redemption of God in my life, total pardon of my sin. To me it was Jesus's way of telling me, "What sin? Stop punishing yourself." The Lord had cast my sins as far as the east is from the west. I now know that he remembers them no more because of the sacrifice of Jesus Christ. With the birth of my son, I finally realized that God is not always holding my sin above my head or trying to remind me of how bad a person I've been. He is not always looking to punish me. While I admit that I still have regret for past mistakes, through this experience I've been able to accept God's forgiveness and forgive myself.

I never felt that I deserved to get married, let alone to have my own children, because of the way I had treated women in past relationships. But in God's grace "deserving" has nothing to do with it. God has blessed me with a beautiful, forgiving wife and three wonderful children. God forgives us and showers grace and mercy upon us because of the sacrifice of Jesus Christ. In return God only asks that we submit our lives to him.

King David was someone who knew of God's grace and mercy first hand. He had sinned greatly, but he had also experienced God's great forgiveness. This David, a forgiven sinner like me, wrote, "as far as the east is from the west, so far has he removed our transgressions from us. As a father has compassion on his children, so the LORD has compassion on those who fear him" (Ps 103:12–13). What's in the past is in the past. You can't change it, but there is redemption for those who humbly repent. God can restore the years the locusts have eaten (Joel 2:25). If you surrender your life to God, he can give you back many times more than Satan stole away from you, as evidenced in the life of Job (Job 42:10–12). Christ can redeem, restore, and renew your life.

Yes, I know and believe God has graciously forgiven me. Still, there are still deep wounds left by sin that may never fully heal while

I am on earth. Feeling remorse for our sin is not necessarily a bad thing. It is a reminder to us of what we should not do. Once you hammer a nail into a piece of wood, even if you remove the nail, there will still be a hole. Even for a man, abortion is not something that's easy to deal with—you never really get over it. To this day, over twenty years later, when I hear the word "abortion" it's piercing to my ears and hurts like a high-pitched screeching sound. I cringe and quickly want to rid it from my mind. I don't do well in conversations regarding abortion, always excusing myself or changing the subject, never commenting on it. I've never felt like I could protest or take a stand against abortion because I would be such a hypocrite and a phony. This is a story that I never wanted to share publicly. I'm not proud of it and really ashamed, but perhaps by sharing it my story can be used to help encourage someone else who is struggling. Opening up about my sin has afforded me liberty to speak more openly about the subject and given me an opportunity to help others make better decisions than I made. Still, my own healing process has been slow and long and will most likely never be complete because there are still emotional scars that will remain as long as I live. Sin always has a price. Someone has wisely said, "Sin will take you further than you want to go, keep you longer than you want to stay, and cost you more than you want to pay."

There are times when I think about what my aborted son might have looked like and what he might have become. He never had the chance. Never had the chance to run and play. Never had the chance to learn and shine. And he never had the chance to do something great for God. I took those opportunities away from him. One day when I enter heaven he will be one of the first people I seek out to meet, and I will hug him tight.

There is hope in Christ for life after bad choices. I pray that you will make better decisions than I've made. But if you've stumbled, know that there is hope through Jesus Christ. No matter what you've done or how bad you've been, by humbling yourself, repenting of your sin, and making Jesus the Lord of your life, God can redeem, restore, and renew your life. It's not about the greatness of your sin, but the greatness of God's salvation and power.

5

~

Forgiven for His Glory

Carmen Pate

". . . Christ Jesus came into the world to save sinners, of whom I am the foremost. But I received mercy for this reason, that in me, as the foremost, Jesus Christ might display his perfect patience as an example to those who were to believe in him for eternal life." (1 Tim 1:15–16 ESV)

As a woman who chose to abort two of her children, I can relate to Paul, who called himself the "foremost of sinners." Another translation says the "worst" of sinners. This is not a label, but a declaration—"If God can save me, then there is hope for everyone!" It was for this reason Christ came, to save sinners. Christ's death on the cross paid the penalty for my sins past, present, and future. In other words, Christ knew before I was even born that I would one day choose abortion, not once but twice. His shed blood cleansed me from all unrighteousness. "Amazing love, how can it be that Christ, my King, would die for me?"

I had believed that my choices were justified; after all, abortion was legal. But even in my brokenness, I knew I had sinned against God. And I knew my life was different when my eyes were opened to the truth about the sin of abortion. Now I live in awe of this Jesus who loved me even unto death. I love much, because I have been forgiven much. My life has been transformed, not unlike the forgiven woman described in Luke 7, who had lived a very sinful lifestyle until she was touched by the Master. My life is now his, to be used for his purposes and for his glory.

When God saved me I knew I had been forgiven, because I felt free for the first time in my life. Once I was set free to be the person God designed me to be, I experienced a change in my heart's desires. I wanted to know this Jesus who had transformed my way of thinking. I began to read and study God's word daily. I was amazed that I understood what I was reading. I learned that it was God's Spirit, the Holy Spirit, who was teaching me, correcting me, growing me into the likeness of Christ. This was the most exciting discovery I had ever experienced. I wanted more!

I began praying and journaling my prayers, asking God to lead me in his path, since I knew that, in my flesh, I would not stay on the correct one. I wanted to be a voice for truth on the sanctity of life, because so many women believe the lies of the enemy. By his grace, I now see that he wanted me to experience first-hand the blessings and tears of working on the front line at a pregnancy care center. When I received a call at my office from a local pastor, I knew the opportunity was from God. I had only met this pastor once, as I exited the door of his church one Sunday morning.

At the time, I was employed by a major grocery retailer and had a very successful career. The pastor sounded almost apologetic when he called, explaining that he wasn't sure why he was calling because I probably had a very good job. But he went on to say the words that changed the direction of my life: "Carmen, I felt led by God to call you and tell you that a local pregnancy center is in need of a director. Would you be interested?" There was no doubt in my mind that God had used this pastor to lead me on the first of many adventures to fulfill God's purpose for my life.

God doesn't waste anything. Looking back, I can see the lessons I learned in every location he has placed me. I had extensive media training and opportunities to interface with media during my retail career. This experience prepared me to help not only the local pregnancy center I directed, but other centers in the country. When crisis media intervention was needed as a result of unwarranted bad press against centers across the country, my media training enabled me to meet that need. What a blessing it was to be of help, as I had already been blessed through the center's post-abortive Bible studies and training. God was allowing me to be healed and to use my gifts and talents to help others at the same time!

God spoke clearly again only a few years later. While on a trip to Israel my husband Bob and I both expressed our feeling that God was getting us ready to move from the home where we had lived for over ten years. I sensed that our move would be for a position God had for me, and Bob and I were in agreement that we would go where God led. Upon our return from Israel, I was going through the stack of mail that had accumulated in our absence and found a magazine from an organization I had never heard of: Concerned Women for America. Bob saw my confused expression and said, "It's a Christian women's organization. I thought you would be interested and so I signed you up!"

As I quickly flipped through the magazine, my eyes landed on an ad. The organization was searching for a vice president of communications. Interested individuals with a master's degree in communications were asked to submit their resumes. Knowing I did not have the required degree, I asked my husband if he thought I should apply anyway. I also pointed out that the job was in Washington, D.C. Bob, always my biggest supporter, enthusiastically said yes. I sent in my résumé and CWA sent me a job description which, to my amazement, aligned perfectly with my experience and skills. Again, God doesn't waste anything! I was hired. Within six weeks, Bob and I moved to Washington, D.C.

This exciting adventure in our nation's capital gave me the rare opportunity to lobby Congress for pro-life legislation, to host press conferences in support of pro-life bills, to co-host a nationally syndicated radio program where life issues were paramount, and to serve as a media spokesperson on behalf of family and life issues. I was promoted to president of the organization after only one year, and my exposure to Congress and the media only increased. It was an amazing journey!

I know I can do nothing apart from Jesus Christ. Please understand that he took a very ordinary, broken vessel, one who was willing to be led by his hand, and to be used by him for life. I am humbled when I think about this, because he and I know how very dependent I am upon his supernatural power working in and through me, as I yield to his Holy Spirit. This same power is available to all who believe in Jesus as their personal Savior and Lord of their lives.

I thought this assignment would be for a lifetime, but I have learned since that life is a journey and we don't arrive at the destination until we go to be with the Lord for eternity. God took me from Concerned Women for America and for a five-year period I was self-employed, speaking at pro-life banquets and conferences, writing pro-life articles, teaching Bible studies, counseling post-abortive women, working in Christian radio, and waiting for the next assignment.

Looking back, I see now that this was a period of learning and growing in intimacy with the Lord. As with most people, my life has had its share of hardships and disappointments. God knew I needed to learn more about trusting and submission to authority. I needed to grow in biblical wisdom and discernment. The five years that I might have perceived as being placed on the shelf were actually years of being purified by fire. I would not trade those years for anything.

God's next calling for me was also very clearly of him. My husband had been betrayed by a business partner and was in the process of losing his business, a manufacturing company, when he became very ill. After major surgery, Bob was homebound for almost a year. During that time he was severely depressed, and felt he could trust no one to run his business . . . except me. Because I had over seventeen years of management experience, and knew his business well after twenty years of marriage, I told him I would run his plant through the bankruptcy and sale of the business. The plant was out in the middle of nowhere in Georgia. My hour-long commute each day was spent crying out to the Lord for wisdom, strength, protection, and guidance. God is faithful to hear our prayers when we ask according to his will.

One day I received a call on my cell phone, which normally did not get reception in the plant office. The call was from Mary Maddoux, the wife of the late Marlin Maddoux, founder and host of the nationally syndicated radio program *Point of View*. When I first came back to the Lord following my abortions, I listened to Marlin Maddoux every day on my commute from work. That program allowed me to learn a lot about the biblical perspective on life issues. Then, while president of CWA, I was honored to be a guest on Marlin's program. That had been almost five years before this call, so I was quite surprised to receive it. My first question was, "Mary, how in the world did you find me?"

In her sweet Texas voice she replied, "Honey, God helped me find you." She then told me that Marlin had gone home to be with the Lord only months before. She also told me that my name had been mentioned as a potential co-host with Kerby Anderson. Things were wrapping up for us in Georgia. God had miraculously sold our home, and we were available for God to move us to Texas. His timing is always perfect.

For the next five years, God allowed me to provide a platform for experts, authors, theologians, and ordinary folks to share biblical truth across the airwaves. Often our guests were pro-life leaders, or post-abortive women sharing their testimonies. We aired programs on adoption and abstinence, alerted our audience to pro-life legislation, and encouraged them to make calls and write letters to congressional leaders. And we talked about the sanctity of life from conception to natural death while challenging our listeners to protect life.

It was during this time that I received a volunteer opportunity. Again, there was no mistaking that the opportunity was God-led. We were living in College Station, Texas, at the time, and I flew to South Dakota to help with the ballot effort in that state to ban abortion. Taking a break to meet some of the many volunteers, I came across a table of very enthusiastic college students. I introduced myself and asked where they were from. You guessed it, Texas A&M . . . in College Station, Texas. We laughed at this "small world" incident and I told their group leader, Shawn Carney, that I was available to help back in Texas at the Coalition for Life he directed. Shawn told me there was someone else I should meet. He later introduced me to David Bereit. David lived in Virginia, but was originally from the Bryan/ College Station area, and had been the founder of Coalition for Life.

Months later, back in Texas, I ran into Shawn and David in the local coffee shop. They said they were just discussing contacting me because they were hoping to get a few pro-life leaders together for a conversation about conducting a national campaign, consisting of forty days of prayer and fasting to end abortion in America. Of course I was interested! I invited the group to my home for our first meeting, where the plans were laid out. I learned that in 2004 Bryan/ College Station's Coalition for Life had led a similar campaign locally with great success. As a result, abortion rates plummeted by 28 percent, and the community earned the reputation of being "the most pro-life community" in the nation.

Other cities began to ask how to replicate this successful campaign. It now made sense to plan a national campaign in which numerous cities could participate simultaneously. The first national 40 Days for Life campaign was launched in the fall of 2007. It has been a great blessing for me to serve on the board of this campaign that is now international in scope. Cumulative results for the ten coordinated campaigns between the fall of 2007 and spring of 2012 include 440 cities that have participated in all fifty states and fourteen countries around the world; more than 525,000 people have joined the effort; 5,928 reported lives have been saved from abortion; twenty-three abortion facilities have shut down; and sixty-nine abortion workers left the industry. This is God's campaign. Those of us who are blessed to serve him in this ministry marvel at his hand of favor seen in the miracles he is working in hearts and minds around the world to end abortion.

Another significant event occurred in 2007—Dr. D. James Kennedy went home for eternity. The founder of Evangelism Explosion, Coral Ridge Ministries, and pastor of Coral Ridge Church, Dr. Kennedy was well known for speaking boldly from the pulpit on moral issues of the day, including abortion. His shepherd's heart had spoken to my heart many times about the sin of abortion, and about God's amazing mercy and grace for those who have walked that path. I was saddened to learn that Dr. Kennedy would no longer be a voice from the pulpit on the sanctity of life. So when I received a call to consider becoming a member of the Coral Ridge Ministry team, I was honored to help carry on Dr. Kennedy's godly legacy. In January of 2012, we launched *Truth That Transforms Radio*—a talk show designed to carry the gospel and a biblical worldview on life issues across the airwaves.

As executive producer and host, I have the privilege of providing a platform for truth for our audiences. Boldly speaking about many issues of the day, the sanctity of life issue remains a priority for our program, as well as for our ministry, now called Truth in Action Ministries. God will carry on Dr. Kennedy's work, and he will carry on the work that you and I leave behind, through others who follow in our steps.

Having been redeemed and set free from the shackles of my sin, I refuse to simply wear the label "post-abortive woman." I am a child of the King of kings, who has been forgiven much for the sin of abortion, as well as many other sins. God continues to heal and restore my life as his Spirit works to transform me into Christ's likeness. God has called me to speak truth to the nation, and though I am certainly not worthy to serve him, I will rely on his Holy Spirit, and be obedient to the call as long as I have breath. Perhaps through me, God may display his perfect patience, so that others may believe and receive eternal life.

We are all in the "lifesaving" business, and though God may place you in different circles of influence than mine, there will always be a life that is waiting for his touch through you. May he find each of us faithful to reach out to the least among us with the same compassion we have been shown.

6

~

Sidewalk Counseling: An Unexpected Job Becomes an Unexpected Adventure[1]

Lauren Muzyka

It was the summer of 2006 and I wanted to find a job serving coffee. I was heading to law school that fall, and I had been told that it would be the three hardest years of my life. "So, buckle up," said my friends who were already there. "You'd better have fun now!" It was a little unnerving, so I set my sights on having some serious fun. I decided I would serve coffee at Starbucks.

The job would be fitting, because in college I was known as "the Starbucks girl." If my friends didn't find me in the student center of my college church, they found me in a local coffee shop. When I thought about it, I honestly couldn't imagine a more perfect summer: I'd be serving up cappuccinos and americanos, and hanging out with my wonderful boyfriend and friends in the North Dallas area.

Early in the summer, I turned in applications at several different coffee shops in my area and attended a handful of interviews. I remember a number of managers patting me on the back, saying, "You'd be a great addition to our team . . . we'll give you a call back!" But then, three weeks went by and . . . nothing. I would call back and ask them, "Have you decided? Any news?" All I got back were a plethora of odd responses. One location lost my application.

Another fired their manager. Others had other random excuses. There I was—with a BA from Texas A&M University in political science and Spanish, plus a graduate certificate in international affairs and a wealth of leadership experience—and I couldn't get a job in a coffee shop to save my life.

It was getting well into June when money was running out, and I got frustrated. I went to my boyfriend, Peter, to ask what I should do. It was actually his mother who suggested that I go to the local diocesan pro-life committee (known as the "Catholic Pro-Life Committee of North Texas" or "CPLC") in Dallas to see if they had any legal work for me.

I'm heading to law school to be a pro-life attorney anyway. Maybe I'm called to get started a bit earlier, I thought.

So I called the organization and a nice woman answered. When I told her that I was heading to law school that fall and wanted to do some pro-life legal work for them, she asked about my prior experience in the pro-life movement. I told her that I had been involved with an interdenominational organization called the Coalition for Life in Bryan, Texas, where I had gone to college. The Coalition for Life, under the leadership of David Bereit, was known throughout the country for its incredible year-round "stand and pray" program, where volunteers covered the local Planned Parenthood abortion facility in prayer during business hours. The Coalition for Life was also renowned for its peaceful and prayerful sidewalk counseling program, where trained volunteers would offer the women going into the abortion center loving alternatives. I had been trained under that organization as a regular prayer volunteer and sidewalk counselor.

Under the leadership of the Coalition for Life, I had the great privilege of experiencing the very first 40 Days for Life campaign, which had been introduced to our college community in the fall of 2004. I remember what life was like on the sidewalk in front of the abortion facility before the 40 Days for Life campaign. On mornings designated by Planned Parenthood as "abortion days," many faithful would gather outside the fence to protest the loss of our preborn brothers and sisters. I remember many praying, yet there were many other "characters" who showed up on our side of the fence on those sad, dismal mornings. I remember the guy dressed up as the grim reaper, pacing back and forth in front of the fence, as if trying to remind our community of the loss of life. I remember a man who used to stake a pole in the ground on the public right-of-way in front of the abortion center and raise the American flag, as if to say he couldn't believe this was legal in our country. And I remember a woman—someone whom I sometimes stood next to while sidewalk counseling—who displayed an aborted child about twenty times larger than life on a huge poster board. I knew she had good intentions and simply wanted to remind people about the truth of abortion.

But I also remember what sidewalk counseling was like on many of those "abortion mornings." It was a rare occasion when anyone would come to the fence when I called out to them. You see, even though I was very peaceful and prayerful in my personal approach, looking back, I realized that I was guilty by association. I saw just how much we—collectively—looked like a circus! We were apprehensive, disorganized, and fearful. Honestly, in the years leading up to that first 40 Days for Life campaign, we didn't know what to do. We didn't know how to respond to the problem of abortion in our community. We didn't know how to deal with the fact that we knew we were losing members of our human family at this Planned Parenthood in our little college town. But looking back now, I'm not sure I blame any woman in a crisis pregnancy for not coming over to talk to me at the fence—they were scared and confused. Why would they approach a circus of people and feel safe pouring their hearts out to me or any other sidewalk counselor?

It wasn't until the fall of 2004 when the leadership of the Coalition for Life—namely, David Bereit, Shawn and Marilisa Carney, and another volunteer named Emily—realized they weren't having much effect on the rate of abortions in our community. They responded by gathering around an old wooden table to pray for an hour. Knowing how it grieves God any time innocent life is taken by our hand, they simply asked him what they could do to end abortion in our community. It was during that hour of prayer that the Lord laid on their hearts the idea of "40 Days for Life"—namely, that they should turn to back to God with prayer and fasting during a constant forty-day prayer vigil in front of the local abortion facility (yes, even twenty-four hours a day!). And they were to ask fellow believers to join them in their efforts.

Gradually, the odd techniques used on "abortion morning" in front of that Planned Parenthood center dissipated. They were replaced by a presence that was more peaceful, prayerful and purposeful than anything we had ever seen. I have fond memories of going out to that first 40 Days for Life vigil to take prayer hours and continue the constant prayer presence during the day and late at night. My boyfriend, Peter, and friends from our church came with me. It was incredibly inspirational to be part of something that was so obviously transforming things on our side of the fence; but even more so, I noticed that this clarion call to prayer was transforming our whole community. We learned later that after that first 40 Days for Life in Bryan, Texas, the abortion rate in our community dropped by 28 percent! I also noticed that more women were coming to the fence to talk, both on abortion days and non-abortion days. This transformation in the faithful pro-life community was my shining example.

I shared highlights of all this with the woman who took my information at the CPLC in Dallas. She thanked me and said they would give me a call back.

The person who called me back was a woman named Carol. She said that she was their sidewalk counseling director.

"You used to sidewalk counsel, right?" she asked. "Yes," I told her. She said, "Lauren, we are in desperate need of sidewalk counselors.

We try to cover all six Dallas area abortion centers with a couple of sidewalk counselors during business hours, and we are short. Would you consider sidewalk counseling full-time with us?"

I hesitated. After all, there was no way I could volunteer full-time and survive without a job.

"Carol, I'm sorry, I would love to help, but I really need a full-time job to make ends meet this summer and prepare for law school."

"No, no, Lauren, we'll cover that. We can give you a stipend for the summer."

I stopped. I didn't know what to say. After all, it didn't fit with anything I was hoping to do that summer. Sidewalk counseling full-time didn't exactly fit into my idea of "fun."

"Do you mind if I think and pray about it and give you a call back, Carol?"

"Sure," she said. We thanked each other and hung up.

Unsure of what to do, I called Peter and asked what he thought. I also felt bad for taking money for something I used to do as a ministry.

Peter said something I will never forget. He said, "Sweetheart, maybe God has different plans for you this summer. And don't feel bad about taking the money—because you wouldn't be able to survive AND serve in this role anyway."

That hit me like a ton of bricks. Maybe I was so wrapped up in my own ideas that I wasn't seeing how God was leading me down a very special path.

I called Carol back and accepted the position.

I knew I would likely have more contact with clients this time, knowing the easier access via public sidewalks in Dallas, as well as the very peaceful prayer presence that the CPLC promoted for sidewalk counseling. Because I finished college and my graduate certificate soon after 40 Days for Life showed up, I had done the bulk of my sidewalk counseling before the atmosphere on the sidewalk had become so much more conducive to conversations with the women visiting the abortion center. As I mentioned before, it was almost impossible to speak to a woman on a Planned Parenthood "abortion morning" due to the tense atmosphere; additionally, we didn't have great access to the clients because of the set-up of the clinic. If a woman was willing to speak to us, she had to take it upon herself to ignore the Planned Parenthood escorts (those designated by the abortion center to walk over to clients after they parked and engage them in conversation so they wouldn't talk to us), cross the parking lot, and walk over to the fence. Due to these circumstances, I had only successfully spoken to a handful of clients during my time in college. Still, I carried the transformative, peaceful, prayerful example of 40 Days for Life into my adventure that summer and beyond.

Days after accepting the new position, I watched the CPLC training video as a "refresher course" for sidewalk counseling. I hit the pavement in the hot Dallas sun every day, traveling between the six area abortion facilities, and—peacefully and prayerfully—offering loving alternatives to women and families who were going into the abortion center.

I had no idea just how much that summer would change my life.

Miracle after miracle occurred before my eyes due to the power of the grace and love that I offered through Jesus Christ. I found my love—or really, God's love—for people growing by leaps and bounds. Even more, I saw that my heart was changing. My new post was purifying me in a powerful way. I found that I had a great love and concern in my heart, so much in fact that I would often pass by people in the grocery store or at church and wonder what their unique story was. After all, I was walking up to total strangers on the sidewalk and offering them loving alternatives to a choice that I knew could affect them for the rest of their life; I was entering their lives at a critical crisis point. I remember one of my fellow sidewalk counselors, Joanne, saying, "You know, it's not the baby that's the problem, it's the situation they're in. The baby simply shines a light into the area of their life that needs help." I came to see that it was only the love of God that could bridge that gap. I was called to be the hands and feet of Christ; I was called to help stand in the gap.

One special "save" that I witnessed was a seventeen-year-old girl who was heading to the abortion facility with her mother in the driver's seat. I was standing in the public alleyway of the abortion center, as cars were beginning to file into the center's parking lot. I leaned down toward one car, and the girl's mother rolled down the passenger side window.

"Hi, my name is Lauren," I said. "We just wanted you to know that we love you, we've been praying for you, and we have real help this morning."

With those simple words, I put a rosary in her hands. In truth, I found out later that she was Pentecostal, not Catholic. But it didn't matter. To her, it was a symbol of prayer. With just a few words and that one gesture, she began to cry.

I began to explain to them about all the help that was available at the pregnancy resource center next door—that we were a community of faith and love, and we would help them with anything they might need.

"But she's so young!" her mother said, bewildered. I could tell they didn't know what to do. Ironically, they felt as if they had no choice.

"But that's why she needs you right now," I gently replied. "She needs your support to do the right thing." I turned back to the young girl and asked, "Do you have a place to live, sweetheart?"

"Yes," she said through her tears.

"Do you have food?"

"Yes."

"Do you have a car?"

"No, but my mom does."

"Then you have more things than many women who have their babies. I have seen women choose abortion—people in my own family, as well as friends—and I have seen the incredible pain that comes with it. So many of them later regretted their decision."

"I have friends who have had abortions. They *all* regret it," she responded.

She was beginning to connect the dots. Mom, daughter, and I kept chatting. Before I knew it, the tears turned to a smile. This young mother began to see how it was possible—even wonderful—for her to choose life.

Suddenly, something happened that I will never forget. The young girl opened the door of the car, jumped out, and threw her arms around my neck. "Let's go get a sonogram!" she exclaimed. I was in awe of the transformation that had just taken place! "You're like an angel!" her mother exclaimed to me.

I sure didn't feel like one—I was shocked myself! Then I realized that I shouldn't be—after all, I knew that with God, all things were possible! I felt the presence of the Holy Spirit in such an incredible way that it was like electricity pulsating throughout my body. I walked the young mother and the grandmother of this preborn child up the stairs to the pregnancy resource center next door, captivated by the incredible blessing of experiencing this moment, due solely to the grace of God. I left these two women in the very capable hands of staff at the center, having congratulated them, and quickly went back downstairs to my post on the sidewalk.

Sometime after the women had left, the counselor at the pregnancy resource center told me that after she walked the two women back to a counseling room, put on their intake video and began to walk away, she heard something odd. She said she heard both mom and daughter start laughing . . . and it continued throughout the video! The counselor stopped and actually thought, *Wait . . . what video did I put in the VCR?* Later, in their counseling session, she learned that both women were so happy they hadn't chosen abortion that they were literally laughing from relief! They were so grateful;

the stress was just rolling off them! Knowing what the Scriptures say about joy, I knew the Holy Spirit had been among us.

When daughter and mom came downstairs after their session, they shared that the pregnancy resource center had given them a pair of baby booties—a sign of hope—with a second appointment to come back and see the ultrasound of her preborn child.

Randomly, I thought, "I bet she's having a girl." We traded information and said goodbye through big smiles, with a promise to keep in touch.

Later that summer, I transitioned from my home state of Texas to my new home in Michigan for the next three years to attend law school. When I finally completed my first semester and headed home to Dallas on break, I decided to call the two women that I had met just months earlier.

I spoke that evening with "Grandma," the mother of the young girl I had spoken with months before. She shared some exciting news with me: "Lauren, Jaala was born on December 27. She is the most beautiful baby I've ever seen. I cannot believe we almost aborted her." What a gift those words were to me. What a gift they were to God!

Soon after, the CPLC called the family and offered to throw a celebratory baby shower for them. Carol, the sidewalk counseling director, emailed me pictures of mom and baby Jaala from the event, just after I had begun my second semester of law school. I treasured those pictures, and when my law school studies got tough over the next couple years, I often pulled those pictures out and reminded myself of why I was there.

I often thought back to that fateful summer and wonder: *What if I hadn't been there? What if I had insisted on my own plans, rather than surrendering to God's? Would Jaala be here? What about the other miracles I experienced?*

Oh, I knew that it hadn't been "me"—after all, my words don't usually make people jump out of cars and hug me! I knew that it had been the Holy Spirit, the great Counselor, who had worked through me, time after time out on that sidewalk. I had only said, "Yes, Lord, use me." But the thought had occurred to me: *What if we each failed to say yes? What if we hadn't been willing to unselfishly give of our time—sometimes in the wind, rain, and heat—to offer loving alternatives to women so that lives might be saved?* In reality, when a child is spared, two lives are saved, because that woman is also spared a lifetime of regret from choosing abortion. And in truth, when you save one, you have saved generations.

I remember my own mother saying to me once, "But Lauren, why do *you* have to be out there? Can't someone else go out?" I understood, naturally, that she was worried about my safety, as any mother would be.

But I remember responding to her, "Mom, if everyone said that, then would anyone go? If not me, then who?"

I look at the picture of sweet baby Jaala—who was very close to becoming another statistic—and realize that every sacrifice I made to be on the sidewalk that summer was worth it.

7

Save the 1: Is Rape a Good Excuse for Abortion?

Rebecca Kiessling

I was adopted nearly from birth, and like many adoptees, I dreamed for years of meeting my birth mother. I thought that meeting my birth family might help me to find my value, identity, and purpose—where I fit into this world.

At the age of eighteen, upon receiving my "non-identifying information," I learned that I was conceived out of rape. I remember feeling ugly, unwanted, and very much devalued and targeted by our society. I instantly thought of what people say about abortion: "I'm pro-life—well, except in cases of rape," or, "I'm pro-choice—especially in cases of rape!" I realized that there were multitudes of people who didn't even know me but were standing in judgment of my life, and who were quick to dismiss it just because of how I was conceived. I felt like I was now going to have to justify my own existence, that I would have to prove to the world that I shouldn't have been aborted and that I was worthy of living. I wanted to have all of my assets lined up so that people would see me as a person of value at a time in my life when I felt like I was being devalued every day.

I ended up in controlling and abusive relationships, until I was beaten up by a boyfriend from law school. He broke my jaw and I eventually lost my front tooth, despite numerous efforts to try to save it. But once when I was speaking at a banquet in Alabama an expert in cosmetic dentistry came up to me afterward and offered to restore all of my teeth for free—not just a bridge with a fourth to match, but eight teeth with porcelain veneers!

I share this story because it's another example from my life of a time when something truly awful happened, but then something beautiful came out of it. Isn't that what God is famous for? The worst evil that man has in store, God can take and use for good, for his glory. It's the story of Joseph in Egypt, and it's the story of our Savior. The story doesn't have to end with the violence having the victory.

I am very thankful that I have this nice new set of teeth, but let me make one thing clear—that does not make me pro-domestic violence. In just the same way, being thankful for my life does not make me pro-rape. I have had people actually say that to me—especially on university campuses during Q & A. They'll say, "Oh, so what you're saying is that if abortion had been legal, you wouldn't be here today. Well, if your birth mother hadn't been raped you wouldn't be here today either, so does that mean that you're pro-rape?" I explain to them that there is a huge moral difference between rape and abortion. In the second situation, I already did exist, and my life would have been ended if I had been killed through a brutal abortion. I may not look the same as I did when I was four years old, or four days old yet preborn in my mother's womb, but that was still undeniably me, and I would have been killed—that's a huge moral difference.

At age nineteen, about six months after learning I was conceived in rape, I did get to contact my birth mother. She filled me in on some horrific details that I was totally unequipped to hear. She was a very petite—4'10" and ninety pounds—single mom heading to the grocery store at night, just down the street from her home. She told me that her attacker had jumped out of the bushes with a knife and abducted her. She went on to describe for me in graphic detail how he brutally raped her every way possible—and that's how I was conceived.

This was so hard for me to hear for several reasons. First of all, after hearing that I was conceived out of a truly worst-case scenario, I just felt totally worthless—like garbage, because of the people who would say that my life was indeed like garbage. I felt like I was disposable. Then I had to realize that my biological father is a really bad man. My birth mother said the police knew he was a serial rapist. She had gone to several police line-ups, but stopped going because she said she wouldn't recognize his face. Lastly, all of these years, I had dreamed so much about meeting my mother, and so to hear that she'd been violated like this pained me.

We arranged for me to fly home and meet her on her fifty-first birthday. In the meantime, she sent me photos and a letter. She wrote,

My Dearest Rebecca,

Hoping by now that the shock of finding out all the details of your birth has been forgotten. For that was not a good enough reason for having to give something up as beautiful as you were. Nothing is as precious as a baby. When you carry a baby for nine months and feel that no one loves you, it's hard. But you were so perfect and pretty. After I gave you up, all these years I had nothing of you, no picture, nothing even saying you were part of me. Just the memory of carrying a baby that I hoped one day would try to find her real mother so I could know my baby. I always loved you in my heart. You were always with me in my thoughts, mostly in July.

It seems like a lifetime I know. When I was sick two years ago I thought I would never get to know my little girl. Would you please see if you could get me a copy of the letter you sent to the Oakland County Judge? It made me cry. Also I would like copies of your poems. These are things I would like to read.

It's been a long three weeks—looking forward to our meeting. I didn't know how to express my inner feelings. IT'S SO GREAT . . .

BIG . . . BEAUTIFUL . . . IT'S ALWAYS BEEN MY DREAM. I AM SO HAPPY I AM CRYING.

A love that ate at me for nineteen years, my daughter at last!

With love,

Your Mom, Joann

This was just all of my dreams come true. I felt so affirmed! I flew home and had a wonderful reunion with her. The next day, she had a huge family reunion for me. I got to meet my half-brother, and it was weird to think that we could have grown up together. Years later, I met my half-sister when I flew to Florida for a five-generation photo. I got to room with my grandmother at the time, which was very cool.

After the reunion, I flew back to college and went to a few meetings of Students for Life. I didn't get involved at that point because I didn't feel like I fit in anywhere. But it gave me the courage to call my birth mother and ask her about abortion, because I still needed to know. I was shocked to hear her tell me that if abortion had been legal at the time, she would have aborted me. I asked her, "You don't mean if you had to do it all over again, right?" And she said, "No." Still, I found myself pleading, "But what about everything you said in that letter—'not reason enough to give up something as beautiful as you were?' What about when you were sick two years ago and you told me that the only thing that kept you going was the hope that someday you'd be able to meet me? What about that? You wouldn't have had that." To which she firmly replied, "You don't know what it was like."

Sadly, I know that what she said is true, but I also know that today she's okay. In fact, she's doing great! She's got a wonderful husband, a beautiful home, lots of grandchildren, and despite the utter horror of her saying that to me, I still chose to nurture a relationship with her and to honor the role that she played in my life. Frankly, I thought that if I were just good enough, then she'd change her mind.

By the time she did change her mind six or seven years later, I was at a much better place in my life where I didn't need to hear that for my own well-being, but it was still great to hear! I was with my birth mother when she was making baby clothes for a niece of mine in Florida who was in a crisis pregnancy with my birth mother's first great-grandchild. She said to me, "You know, I'm really glad she decided to have this baby. And by the way, I've changed my mind about all that."

I was born on July 22, 1969. The trial date in *Roe v. Wade* was May 22, 1970, exactly ten months from my birthdate; and the U.S. Supreme Court's opinion was issued on January 22, 1973, exactly three and a half years after my birthdate. So I just barely made it!

Comments That Come My Way

I always try to explain the truth to people: when you identify yourself as "pro-choice," or make that exception for rape, what that really translates into is your being able to stand before me, look me in the eyes, and say to me, "I think that your mother should have been able to abort you." That's a pretty powerful statement. I would never say anything like that to someone. I would never say to someone, "If I had my way, you'd be dead right now." But that is the reality with which I live. I challenge anyone to describe for me how it's not! For most, the exception for rape is just a concept—a quick cliché to avoid the main issue of abortion. I do hope my story, and the dozens of other stories of those conceived in rape or pregnant by rape, can help to put faces, voices, and stories to this issue.

Amazingly, I have had university students raise their hand during the question and answer time after my speech in order to declare, "Yeah, I just want to say that I have no problem looking you in the eyes and stating that I think your mother should have been able to abort you, and I fully understand that it would mean that you'd be dead right now. I just want to say that I have no problem doing that." Wow! So here you go—here are people who, out of their "care for women," would say such a thing to a woman like me. I'm not feelin' the care. Besides, what good is my right to anything as a woman, if I don't have my right to life?

I'm so thankful my life was spared. I know that a lot of well-meaning Christians might conclude, "Well, God really meant for you to be here!" But I also know that God intends for *every* preborn child to be given the same opportunity to be born, and I can't sit contentedly saying, "Well, at least my life was spared," or, "I deserved it!"

I've also had people say, "Oh well! If you'd been aborted, you wouldn't be here today, and you wouldn't know the difference anyway, so what does it matter?" Believe it or not, some of the top pro-abortion philosophers use the same kind of argument: "The fetus never knows what hit it, so it can't miss its life." So I guess if you stab someone in the back while he's sleeping, then it's okay, because he doesn't know what hit him? I'd explain to my classmates how the same logic used to justify abortion would justify "me killing you today, because you wouldn't be here tomorrow, and you wouldn't know the difference anyway—so what does it matter?" They'd just stand there with their jaws dropped. It's amazing what a little logic can do, when you think this thing through, and consider what we're really talking about: there are lives that are not here today because they were aborted. The lives of babies matter. My life matters. Your life matters, and don't let anyone tell you otherwise!

I Have Great Worth—I Am a Child of God

One of the greatest things I've learned is that I'm not a "product of rape," but a child of God. That rapist is NOT my creator, as some people would have me believe. Psalm 68:5–6 declares, "A father to the fatherless . . . is God in his holy dwelling. God sets the lonely in families." Psalm 27:10 tells us, "Though my father and mother forsake me, the LORD will receive me." I know that there is no stigma in being adopted. We are told in the New Testament that it is in the spirit of adoption that we are called to be God's children through Christ our Lord (Rom 8:15). So he must have thought pretty highly of adoption to use that concept as a picture of his love for us—not second best or a last resort, but God's first choice, and meant for the body of Christ.

Most importantly, I've learned, and I can teach my children, that you don't have to prove your worth to anyone. If you want to know what your value is, all you have to do is look to the Cross—because that's the infinite price that was paid for your life! God thought I was pretty valuable—not worthless, but priceless. I hope you know your own worth! When you can say you are pro-life without exception, it's like saying, "I get it. You matter. Yours was a life worth saving." Now I hope you'll go forward from here, and do the same for others!

8

Our Beautiful Daughter with Spina Bifida

Anthony Horvath

It was December of 2006 and my wife and I were giddily awaiting the results of the ultrasound. We had specific requests for God: we wanted a girl, and just *one* girl! You see, we had three boys at this point, and the last two had come as a batch. To this day, I remember the ultrasound technician displaying the two circles on the screen, patiently waiting for it to sink in that we were looking at two heads, that we were expecting twins. It was a shock, to say the least, but not nearly as shocking as coping in a household with three boys running wild.

You can see, then, that as we watched the ultrasound technician at work this third time, we were on pins and needles. We had brought our eldest son with us to share in the experience, and he of course was looking forward to a sister as much as we were looking forward to having a daughter. When the word came that we could expect a girl, we were all grinning ear to ear.

For some reason, though we were jubilant, the technician did not seem to be sharing in our joy as our previous technicians had. His somber silence went unnoticed even as the exam went on longer than we expected. It was only in retrospect that we recalled how subdued and methodical he was.

The retrospection was not long in coming.

The technician ushered us to one of the clinic rooms to await the doctor who strode in not too long afterwards and quite directly gave us the news: "Your daughter has hydrocephalus, and this is most likely the consequence of a condition called spina bifida." It was blunt and to the point, just like that.

The rest, as you can imagine, was a blur. The tone of the conversation changed radically as we sought information. Our eldest, not comprehending the change, continued to be happy and joyful, adding to the surreal nature of the episode. It was quickly determined that we would go to the hospital for a "second level" ultrasound to confirm if our daughter did in fact have spina bifida. The appointment was set up for about two hours from that moment, and we were sent on our way.

If you are unaware of what spina bifida and hydrocephalus entail, you may very well understand the kind of daze that we were in. We had some reference point for spina bifida, since there was a child at church that had the condition. The multitude of related difficulties associated with the condition, where a bit of the spinal column protrudes from the spine, were unknown to us. Hydrocephalus is one of the more visible signs of the condition, perhaps even more so than the protrusion. "Water on the brain," as it was once called, refers to the cerebrospinal fluid which accumulates in the skull, causing it to expand and grow larger. Normally, this fluid is held in balance, being created and disposed of automatically by the body. The protrusion of the spine, however, often results in the shutting of the "valve" that the fluid would normally be disposed through, thus leaving it no escape.

You now know more than we did before that second ultrasound. In the short period of time between the two ultrasound appointments, we attempted to learn as much as we possibly could, turning to the modern era's highest authority in all "knowledge"—Google.

Suffice it to say that time did not allow for any significant examination of the issue. Essentially we learned that, as with many conditions, there can be minor expressions of the condition or there can be extreme ones. To put it another way, there were both "best case scenarios" and "worst case scenarios," with a whole world of possibilities between them. The other thing we learned was vitally important: there was no way of ascertaining which scenario was going to be your life until after the child was actually born. Indeed, in some cases, if not most cases, one could not know how things would go for several years.

It was these two basic facts that we gleaned from our brief window of time to do some research: there were a variety of outcomes and it was impossible to know which outcome would be ours.

Armed with only this information, we met with the "high risk" doctor who handled situations like ours. He set out to spot the "defect" on the ultrasound, because identifying the cause of the hydrocephalus would go a long way towards understanding our predicament. The ultrasound went on and on, because our daughter wouldn't cooperate until a last minute flip—when we were about to give up—showed the defect low on the spine. Lower on the spine made for better prospects than higher on the spine.

We gave the doctor the go-ahead to perform the amniocentesis procedure, which would verify with near 100 percent certainty that in fact our daughter had spina bifida. Moments later, we had our answer. It was a fact, corroborated in three ways: we were expecting a child with spina bifida.

It is hard to put into words what we were feeling at that moment. The feeling was pulled out and extended over the course of a week, and my wife and I experienced it differently. For me, it was as if the child had died, and in some sense, a child had died. It was the daughter I had been expecting that died: the daughter that I would play soccer with in the yard, that would chase butterflies around, that I would watch leave my doorstep on the way to her prom, that

I would walk down the aisle at her wedding. I grieved as though I had experienced a death. Until that moment, I did not know it was possible to grieve without someone really dying. Not understanding what I was going through made it worse. With a death, you understand that you will be going through phases of coping with the grief. For all I knew, I was feeling that moment how I would always feel. My wife was similarly grieved, and together we were thrown into shock.

And then the question came: "Do you want to terminate the child?"

This was the gist of the question posed, not the exact wording. Looking back, I have no qualms with the way the doctor put the matter before us, but that probably has much to do with the fact that I prefer directness whenever I can get it. I do have serious objections to putting such a question to people who have just been stunned in such a way, especially when they have very little information to go on. But it is more than that.

The question can be re-worked to reflect more honestly what it conveys: "Society has agreed that you can get an abortion for just about any reason that you want at almost any time that you want. Society would certainly respect your decision to abort if your child is diagnosed with a birth defect. Your child has been so diagnosed; *so, would you like to kill it?*"

Abortion statistics for terminating children diagnosed with a birth defect such as spina bifida, Down Syndrome, and similar defects are estimated between seventy and ninety percent.

To this day, I have not been more proud of my wife than I was that day when she looked the doctor in the eye and told him that there was no question of us not keeping this child. With the question answered decisively, it did not come up again.

I often wonder how it would have gone if we had wavered. The truth is that we did not make our decision that moment in December of 2006. We had made it together years before then as we worked to integrate the consequences of our faith in Jesus Christ into our real life. Jesus died for all, *even before we were born*. God is the source of Life. God knew us *before creation*. God is the final arbiter of the value of people, not the people themselves. God has also added much to our value by sending his own Son to die and pay a ransom price for us.

These convictions, derived years earlier and applied earnestly as best that we could in the midst of our frailties, made the decision inexorably before the actual moment of decision was upon us.

So, my wife and I chose life. We chose life because *God chose life*. I tell the story in greater detail in my short book *We Chose Life: Why You Should Too*, but even there it must be considered abbreviated. I cannot do justice to the week of bitter despair that followed from first learning about our daughter's condition, but I also cannot do justice to the *full* story, which is one of great joy and happy fulfillment. There came a point where we "sucked it up" and finally laid to rest the child of our expectations and determined to love the actual child in front of us. Even as I write that, it seems a crass way to put it, but I am convinced that part of the problem was having certain expectations in the first place.

It is nowhere written that life will be easy, or that it will go a certain way. Our other children may seem to be "normal," but real life tells us that this can change in a heartbeat. Life can go in any direction at any moment. We have no right to expect bliss. We have no right to expect a painless journey. We have a God who could have "aborted" his creation the moment that it took a turn for the worse. He knows better than us what great suffering has transpired because he chose to see it through to the end. God didn't merely choose life, he chose joy: "*For the joy* set before him he endured the cross, scorning its shame, and sat down at the right hand of the throne of God" (Heb 12:2). There is a joy that is made complete by enduring and passing through suffering. God has proved Jesus's example that suffering, while difficult, *is worth it* in the end. That's the thing about joy—the harder the circumstances, the more pronounced and satisfying it is.

More than five years have passed since we sat in that ultrasound room. What should I tell you? That we have been blessed with the "best case scenario"? Were the doctors wrong? Or, has it been the "worst case scenario"? It is hard, looking back, to know how much weight to give such questions. Some people would say that we are living through the "worst case scenario," but we would do it all over again in a heartbeat.

I can say one thing for sure: my daughter is beautiful. She lights up every room she enters and puts a smile on the face of every person she meets. This is the truth. I cannot begin to tell you what joy she has brought into our lives and the lives of others. She is God's gift to us—exactly as she is. Our journey in parenting has not been easy, but we can confidently declare, *it has been worth it.*

9

Forgotten Fathers

Frank Gray

Growing up, I had a great life. I've always been close to both sides of my family and have always had a ton of friends. We moved around a lot, due to my father's job. But those circumstances taught me three things that would shape my worldview from an early age.

First, moving around for the sake of employment and bettering one's position in a company put a heavy value on money and why it was important to have it. Second, the independence and courage that it took to move around showed that with hard work, by ourselves, we could do anything. And third, we learned not to get attached to our environment or the people in it, for we all knew that we would just move again before too long.

The Bible says, "There is a way that seems right to a man, but in the end it leads to death" (Prov 14:12 ESV). Even though I had a great childhood, I was spiritually dead and blind. I could not see that all the things in life that seemed worth pursuing actually were *not* worthy goals.

I lived in a great home with parents who loved each other. I should have seen God's hand in my family growing up, because we loved each other; yet I did not walk with Christ. We went to church infrequently and I did not fully understand what Christ did on the cross. I was exposed to sex early and, looking back; I can see how it truly affected me in a negative way. At age seven, I found a video in the garage and my curiosity led me to take it to my room and watch. That was my first exposure to pornography. At age eight, I got a TV in my room for Christmas and I was exposed to late-night HBO and Cinemax.

I found watching those acts to be fun and exciting, even at that age. I recall wanting to hurry up and grow older so I could explore the sexual acts that I saw with someone special. Looking back, I can see just how lacking and misguided my life really was without Christ.

As I got older, I still believed that if I did good things, obeyed the law, and listened to my parents, I would live a fulfilling life and God would smile on me. My father was strict so I applied myself to studies and sports. I did well—both in the classroom and on the football field. Drugs, sex, and alcohol were never an issue for me in grade school and high school due to my upbringing. However, when I closely examine my life during those years my imperfections are evident. I did not have sex in high school, but I would sneak girls over to the house and would act inappropriately with them in other ways. I didn't drink or do drugs in high school, but I had a sense of self-righteousness and I was quick to judge any of my peers who sinned.

I was fortunate enough to play Division One football in college and pursued my dream of being a graphic designer. My collegiate football career was not great. I carried the burden of being just a "solid" player, and I was always seeking to demonstrate my worth to my coaches and teammates. I loved the underdog role and always tried to go above and beyond. It was the college football scene that fueled my selfish pride and set me on a path that would lead straight to the cross to ask for forgiveness.

After two years of being dissatisfied with the amount of playing time I was getting, I left school in Ohio and transferred to North Texas. When I arrived, I was very bitter about how things ended in Ohio and was looking for a fresh start.

My next three years at North Texas ended up being worse than in Ohio. There were three games still to play in my senior season when I left the football team and never returned. After abruptly ending my college football career, I now focused all my attention on academics, and saw success there. Unfortunately, focusing on academics would only last so long. I became bored and looked for something to fulfill me. I tried to fill the void with women. This would mark the beginning of the end for a Christ-less Frank Gray.

When my college football days ended I felt alone and was socially awkward. I became almost obsessed with finding a girlfriend. But after a few months in the dating world I became depressed, wishing that there were more to life than hard work. I turned to online dating and decided that I would date the first girl who would talk to me. In three short weeks, I met someone and we quickly became an item. I could have sworn that I was in love, but in fact it was lust.

After dating this girl for two months, I moved into her home with her and her nine-year-old daughter. In a matter of months, I had gone from being a college kid to a father figure with husband-like duties and responsibilities. Obviously, I was not ready for this. While I loved the feeling of independence and responsibility that I had taken on, it was a disaster waiting to happen. My parents were disappointed in me for doing this, but I did not care—it was my life and I was going to do whatever I wanted. At the time, I felt more independent and in control of my life than ever before—in reality, though, that was quite the lie.

We lived together for another six months before a string of fights and arguments led to our breakup, with me moving out of her home. I was shocked and mad at myself, feeling responsible for letting all that hurt happen to everyone involved. I mistakenly believed that the only way to recover was to move on—and quickly.

Three short weeks later I met another girl and we quickly became an item. Once again, I was motivated more by lust than love, so on the night of October 27, 2006, we made our relationship "official" by having sex. Little did we know that on that night, we would conceive a child.

Romans 8:28 says, "We know that in all things God works for the good of those who love him, who have been called according to his purpose." I think about this verse a lot. I still wonder why I chose to end my child's life. My girlfriend and I chose abortion together, simply because we thought a child would be an inconvenience. It was legal, after all, so we convinced ourselves it was OK. I did not believe that it was a child, and my worldview at the time helped make my decision to abort easier.

Yet, deep inside, I knew that it was wrong and I hated God for putting me in that position. Six months after aborting our first child, we discovered that my girlfriend was pregnant again. For me, the choice was easy—abortion. For her, it was not. She actually believed that it was a sign from God that we should keep this baby. When she told me that, I became enraged. I pressured her into ending the life of our second child and I hated her for turning on me. After the second abortion I felt very cold and began to doubt the existence of God. I had tried to live the perfect life and failed miserably. This put me into a deeper depression. Several months after the second abortion, my girlfriend left me.

I began despising women and decided to use them for my own selfish pleasure. After months of doing this, I grew tired of my own self-prescribed routine and decided that women and dating were not for me. It was during this time that I felt a great void. Not knowing what to do, I worked out daily and became a workaholic. I didn't have a lot of friends because I isolated myself from other people.

My life changed in the summer of 2008, when God placed a friend and coworker in my life who lived for Christ. We later became roommates and on our first night in the house, he asked me if I knew Jesus Christ. I lied to him and said that I did. In reality, I had no idea what he was talking about.

But God used him to plant a seed in me that very night. Just before I went to bed, I searched for and found a Bible that my parents had given me. Opening it, I skimmed the pages and something came over me, a feeling that I still can't quite explain. It was the feeling of searching for something and finding it, but being puzzled by the fact that I didn't know what to do with it.

The next day, a Sunday, my roommate and I were introduced to Watermark Church by a mutual friend and coworker. The pastor was preaching a series of messages that examined biblical vs. secular worldviews. He was in the middle of the series that was titled "What in the world are you thinking?" Surely it was in God's plan for me to be a part of that series, because I began to question my last twenty-four years here on earth.

The following Sunday, I started attending Watermark on a fairly regular basis and as my curiosity for the cross deepened, I saw God moving in my life for the first time. On October 27, 2008, two years after conceiving my first child, I gave my life to Christ and was baptized. Psalm 103:12 says, "As far as the east is from the west, so far has he removed our transgressions from us." I thank God for this truth. By sending his Son to die on the cross for my sins, he has freed me from the bondage to sin—including my own abortion transgressions.

Soon after my baptism, I was introduced to a group of guys in my life-stage who were running toward Christ. Since turning my life to Christ, my roommate and I were each other's accountability partners. In February of 2009, my roommate and I joined a community group. Being in community with other men of God changed my life.

During the next few years, as I continued to work through my struggles stemming from the guilt of the abortions along with newly discovered struggles of pride and control, I discovered in a deeper way God's forgiveness and restoration. I also began preparing for marriage—marriage God's way. It would be two years of walking with Christ before I would date again. God used that time to prepare me by building authentic relationships with people, studying his word, and stretching my faith, so that I could know with certainty that his plans for me would be always be the best.

In April 2010, God's providence brought me to Janna, the woman who was to be my fiancée. I had prayed for God to send me someone special, not for my sake, but to bring him more glory. He put a Christ-centered woman in my path who not only loves me, but "sharpens" me daily and makes me a better person for him. He didn't have to bless me this way, but he did and in that I clearly see that his grace does abound.

One of the first Bible verses to really grab my attention was Romans 3:23, "For all have sinned and fall short of the glory of God." It was amazing how such a simple verse told me everything I needed to know about why my perfectionist lifestyle was flawed and unattainable.

The very best I could do on my own was really only like a "filthy garment" before our Holy God (Isa 64:6). The realization that I am a sinner and not able to be perfect on my own terms weighed heavily on my heart. The discovery of Christ and his free gift of righteousness truly lifted that burden. Indeed, his "yoke is easy" and his "burden is light" (Matt 11:30).

Thinking back to Romans 8:28, I now see how God is graciously using my post-abortion experiences for good. Christ saved my life in the midst of desperation and depression, and he is now using it for good. I have parents who now follow Christ, a great group of guys that I'm in community with and I have the privilege of serving children and helping men who have been hurt through a past abortion decision. God is so good and I'm honored to have given my life to him!

In September of 2009, God was not done working in my post-abortion recovery. I heard Carol Everett, a national pro-life speaker, speak at Watermark's Young Adult ministry, and God used that event to encourage me to seek healing. I received that healing at another church, meeting faithfully with a post-abortion support group every Wednesday night for twelve weeks. What God did during that time was nothing short of amazing. During those twelve weeks, I was encouraged enough to talk to my father, roommate, and community group about my abortive past. Before my own post-abortive recovery, I had not told a soul about my experiences with abortion.

I completed the twelve-week program and felt such a burden lifted from me. God moved my heart to share my testimony of finding grace from my past abortion decisions at Watermark's Christmas Eve service that December. During this time, God led me to begin thinking about starting a post-abortion recovery ministry for men. God positioned the right people in my path; together, we began to pray and think through ways to help other men whose past is similar to mine.

In January of 2010, I had the opportunity to speak to three men about their abortion decisions. One of these men would become the first to begin and complete the Forgotten Fathers program at Watermark. Since May of 2010, thirteen men have been introduced to Forgotten Fathers, with seven so far having completed the program. One man, in particular, received Christ through the ministry.

Due to conversations concerning myself and other men who have been a part of Forgotten Fathers, and by the grace of God, three children have been saved in the womb to date.

I'd like to take a few moments to look at Forgotten Fathers. The following three statements define the heart of the ministry.

FORGIVENESS & HEALING: Forgotten Fathers provides a safe place for men to share and discuss their feelings about their role in a past abortion. Having these men understand that they are saved by grace through faith is the first important step. Letting them know that they are forgiven for this transgression is the second. The healing process continues from this point, showing these men that they are truly free from the bondage of a past abortion decision and that they are not alone.

SPIRITUAL GROWTH: Forgotten Fathers encourages and aids members with various opportunities for spiritual growth. The ministry takes an in-depth look at God's point of view on subjects such as forgiveness, anger, and depression. Understanding the character of God as well as God's view on creation and life is also explored.

COMMUNITY: The structure of Forgotten Fathers resembles that of a band of brothers—all sharing, all encouraging and all concerned for one another. Accountability is very important as everyone is responsible for keeping up with one another's well-being. This is especially important to the leader of the ministry. The ministry leader is key in facilitating/leading discussions as well as guiding members through the Bible. Encouraging others is a must for the ministry leader.

To summarize, whether it be my story (which is really God's story) or Forgotten Fathers (which is really God's ministry), one thing is evident: the salvation and restoration of sinful people is God's work. It is even more mind-boggling to think that he uses people like you and me to help in the process of healing others and to execute his will on earth. If God can save and use a man like me, there is hope for any man!

10

Becoming a True Friend
for Mothers at Risk

Julie Rosati

Julie Rosati used to wonder what the big deal was about abortion, but one day she found out how much the issue really matters. One of her housemates seemed to be covering up something, behaving strangely and secretively. Finally, she confided in Julie that she had taken abortion pills, was in great pain, and felt scared. Julie, who felt rather helpless in that situation, then and there promised God to become educated about abortion, to learn his heart on the matter and somehow get involved. Five years later, as a pro-life worker in New York City, Julie has been instrumental in saving the lives of over one thousand children. I was privileged to meet this remarkable lady during a pro-life outreach in Dallas, Texas. Here is her story.
—Julia Pritchett, Sidewalk Advocates for Life

My work began in 2004 as I began volunteering with Expectant Mother Care Pregnancy Centers in the Bronx. The counselor there sort of took me under her wing and "taught me the ropes," so to speak. This occurred after a process of dealing with my own un-certainties about when life begins and re-educating myself with the truth about God's plan for sexual purity and his heart for the preborn and the sanctity of life.

My instructor, Liz, told me I was a natural which was absolutely reassuring because even though I had traveled extensively, I was just a simple country girl and I had never been pregnant. Wasn't I out of my league trying to relate with New York City girls about a subject that I had no personal experience with? "No," Liz encouraged me, "God has given you a gift, and I am so thrilled to see how it will unfold. Please don't give up; these girls and their preborn babies need you." Even though I constantly battled discouragement, I managed to return week after week to Liz's office.

Suddenly one day in 2005, the executive director of EMC called me and offered me a full-time job as a sidewalk counselor backed up by a mobile unit. I prayed for about . . . ten seconds! "Yes!" I told him, "I'll take it! But please, Mr. Slattery, no video cameras and no interviews."

On our first day out pretty much every news station in NYC showed up to mock the unveiling of our van. I even had to do an interview in Spanish for both a local TV station and a newspaper! *So much for my one request*, I mused. God used that initial experience, however, to help me overcome other intimidating situations that would come my way—like an abortion clinic director trying to cast a spell on me, or the clinic making constant false claims to police who then threatened to have me arrested.

After about a year working as a sidewalk counselor, I was asked to manage the interns. I would eventually become a pregnancy center director. It's now 2011, and for the last seven years I have been true to my promise to serve God. In case you think this kind of work is glamorous, let me describe my life.

By choice and financial necessity, I live in a six-by-six "closet" with a twin mattress on the floor. There isn't room for my belongings (not that I keep many). New York City is an extremely expensive place to live and pro-life work pays its rewards in heaven, not necessarily here on earth. I have endured "the closet" because God gave me a "missionary" spirit and he has placed me in the "mission field" created by the legalization of abortion. God has called me to fight on the front lines. I'm not called to give up, stay home, or be silent. Many acquaintances and friends have voiced their opinions on my "missionary" lifestyle. Some will ask me belittling questions. "You went to college for this?" "What about benefits?" "Won't you just end up in jail?" "How many of those girls even change their minds?" "Do you really think you are even making a difference?" "Why don't you focus on teaching kids to be safe and responsible?" "When will you have time for your own family?"

Discouragement is common for sidewalk counselors. I have dealt with it, like all the other counselors, through prayer. Sidewalk counselors are tempted to try to carry the burden themselves; they hurt a lot because they see girls going into a clinic pregnant and then leaving with an empty womb and a lollipop in their mouths. Sometimes the girls walking would ignore the sidewalk counselors and sometimes say something harsh. Other times, a young woman would agree with everything the sidewalk counselor was saying, but then choose to abort. But eventually, we experience the thrill of a turn-around—a mom who chooses life and sticks to her decision.

The bottom line is that we each have to do what we sense is the will of God for our lives. In this kind of work, we can't get all tied up with the results; we are called to serve God and love these needy girls. And God looks for available people. My phone seems to go off every few minutes. I have dozens of women contacting me every week. For some, I might be their only friend. For others, I am their lifeline during a pregnancy that no one around them supports. I receive many pictures of babies walking for the first time, baptism invites, advice requests, and so much more. While this may seem "touching," it's an enormous responsibility. When I have promised these women that I'll "be there," that may mean even meeting at 3:00 AM after spending a draining day at work.

Do I ever feel "burned out?" Certainly. But when my lamp is low, I share what flame I have with someone else. If I do that then

I'll keep my own flame going and help ignite others' flames. I look for young pro-lifers in high schools and college campuses and train them, love them, pour myself into them, and teach others to do my job, so that I can take a much-needed vacation. If God has called you to this work don't leave until it's his appointed time. We cannot lean on our own understanding, but must trust in God with all our heart. He will give us the grace, the compassion, and the power to accomplish his good pleasure.

I must acknowledge that I do have dreams, like any thirty-year-old woman, but I have put my own dreams and goals on hold, trusting that God holds my future and will provide for all my needs. I believe God placed me outside of Dr. Emily's abortion facility for a purpose and that he will move me when it is his time.

I certainly have days of weariness and discouragement. One day after church I was riding my bike home on a major street in the Bronx when I pleaded with God to please allow me the great pleasure of bumping into someone, someday, whom I had met outside the abortion facility. I asked the Lord to please let me see her happy with her baby. In spontaneous anticipation I began scanning the sidewalks and turning my neck from side to side just in case God decided to answer my prayer quickly. Then I saw her. I recognized the lady on the sidewalk pushing her twin boys in a stroller. I had met her twice outside of the abortion facility when she tried to abort, once at fourteen weeks and then again at twenty weeks. I threw my bike down and ran up to them screaming in great joy and shouting her name. After her initial shock, she began to cry and told me she had been looking for me all this time because she wanted me to be the godmother of her twins. She had her two daughters with her, too, and they all kept hugging me. Such encounters can keep me encouraged for a long time!

11

Students for Life

Kristan Hawkins

My earliest memory of being active in the pro-life movement was when I was in elementary school. I remember driving around town with my Mom buying little rolls of Lifesavers candy to decorate our Right to Life float in the Fourth of July parade. That was the first time I witnessed firsthand the "controversy" of the pro-life message. I was riding my bike ahead of the Lifesaver float and wondered why some people were cheering and giving thumbs up and others were booing. The most vivid memory I have is of a woman in her late twenties or early thirties who was actually yelling at my cousin and me as we were riding our bikes. While I wasn't converted to the pro-life view by witnessing the pro-choice woman yell at elementary school kids, the seed of being a pro-life activist was planted.

I became pro-life the day that I walked into AIM Pregnancy Help Center in Steubenville, Ohio, when I was fifteen years old. A typical over-achiever in high school, I was planning to graduate a year early and needed 100 service hours to graduate with honors. A woman at my church mentioned that I should help her at a local women's center. Not fully understanding what I was getting myself into, I eagerly agreed.

The day I walked into AIM, I was expecting to assist my church friend in her accounting work and help women. Little did I know what "helping women" was going to come to mean. I had always thought of myself as pro-life but, in the back of my mind, wondered if abortion would really be that bad if a woman had been raped or if one of my friends should become pregnant.

The women at the Center were so excited by my presence and immediately started training me so I could help talk to clients, the young girls who were coming into AIM. I was given a stack of VHS tapes, brochures to study, and books to read. Books like *Lime 5*, which highlights the dangers of the abortion industry; *Forbidden Grief*, which talks about post-abortion syndrome; and *Pro-Life Answers to Pro-Choice Arguments*, the ultimate pro-life activist guide. Naturally I went for the VHS tapes first and popped in *The Silent Scream*. There on the screen was Dr. Bernard Nathanson explaining that he was a former abortionist, holding the metal instruments, and describing the procedure in detail while an abortion was taking place on the screen. Next, I remember a video of Fr. Frank Pavone holding up little babies who had been placed in caskets after they were aborted by saline infusion late in the pregnancy. I will never forget the look of those little charcoaled babies.

And that was it. That's the day I became not just pro-life but passionately pro-life. Driving home that day, I thought about how I had planned my life: graduate early, get a degree in aeronautical engineering, work for NASA—and how that plan was going to have to change.

My thinking then and now is this: How could anyone see and grasp what abortion really is and not do everything within their power to stop it?

From that first day at AIM Pregnancy Help Center, I threw myself into my work—staying late, volunteering to take on the tough projects, going above and beyond the normal volunteer work for a teenager. Sure, I helped with the accounting, sorted and organized the room with the diaper donations, and cleaned, but I put most of my efforts into trying to make AIM the best center for any woman seeking help—creating a new look for the donor newsletter, thinking of new ideas, and learning how to counsel women myself. By the end of the summer I was ready, or so I thought, to go back to my high school and make a difference. Before the school year even started, I organized a meeting with my principal, and wrote a letter about why a pro-life organization was needed at my school. I was thrilled when I was allowed to organize Teens for Life. That school year was the most difficult of my life. In order to graduate early, I had to double up on some of the toughest subjects, take all of the standardized tests, and apply to college. On top of that, since I had become involved in the pro-life movement, I began to watch a new cable news station, Fox News, and was enthralled and instantly hooked, seeing the connection between politics and the pro-life movement. I changed my proposed major from engineering to political science.

And I soon found that starting a Teens for Life group in my conservative, blue collar, Democratic hometown wasn't going to be as easy as I thought. Teachers would single me out in class and rumors began to spread among the students. To compound my situation, I was a new pro-lifer—passionate and unwilling to compromise in my beliefs, but sadly, not always a good listener.

Throughout the year, my skills as a pro-life student apologist began to improve. Other students joined the Teens for Life group and I became involved with my local pro-life community. The local Right to Life group was excited to see me join their monthly meetings, while the statewide group, West Virginians for Life, was eager to get me involved speaking statewide to other Teens for Life groups. They even allowed me to tag along when lobbying at the West Virginia Capitol. I was so fortunate that every adult I worked with at AIM and in the local and state pro-life groups was excited by my presence and welcomed my creative, new ideas.

Just a few months after I became involved with Brooke County Right to Life, the governor, Bob Wise, was set to visit my high school and hand out state scholarships. This pro-abortion governor had just vetoed our state Woman's Right to Know Act, and I wanted to make sure pro-lifers were there to greet him as he entered my high school. However, I couldn't participate in the protest as I had to be at the governor's ceremony, since I was slated to receive a scholarship. So I organized the protest, made the signs, and solicited my family and friends to greet the governor in front of the school while I was in class. I had no cell phone to stay updated on the progress but my mom did have the special honor of holding the "Governor Wise Isn't So Wise" sign in front of the school. I would have liked to have seen his face.

Battle-tested from high school, I hit the ground running when I entered Bethany College that fall. I quickly found an advisor, the Catholic priest assigned to the school, and launched Bethanians for Life. Of course, my liberal, pro-abortion professors didn't let these actions go unnoticed in my small political science classes of fifteen or twenty students. Almost immediately after I got the group approved by our student government—no small feat—a pro-abortion group called Bethanians for Sex started on campus.

It was a lonely road some days. Instead of inviting me to join their clubs, entire fraternities and sororities threw popcorn at my pro-life display table in the cafeteria. I lived in constant fear that my pro-abortion professors would hold my views against me when it came time for my subjective grades. I studied harder than any of my classmates as my professors frequently called on me to answer difficult questions and defend my "illogical" conservative beliefs. My work did not go unnoticed as I was selected as the top political science student my senior year, became a fellow of the department, and graduated with a 4.0.

I worked at the Republican National Committee (RNC) right out of college and then as a political appointee at the U.S. Health and Human Services (HHS) Center for Faith-Based and Community Initiatives. I thought I was set—I had an ideal job, one that many young Republicans aspired to. But shortly after I started, I was turned off by the lack of pro-life values I found there. As much as I wanted to work full-time in the pro-life movement, I thought only "older people" with established careers and degrees could do that, not some girl who had just graduated college. I didn't know of any pro-life groups out there except for National Right to Life and didn't think there was anywhere for me to fit in.

While working at Health and Human Services in an attempt to de-polarize my résumé before applying to what I knew would be a hostile graduate program, I took my grad school exams, prepared my applications and narrowed down my list of schools. I also married the man whom I had been dating since my freshman year in high school—and who had witnessed my transformation into a pro-life activist.

Working for the government was a sweet job with easy duties, normal hours, and good pay and benefits, but I was so bored and I hated it. Every day I looked for job openings in Washington, D.C. I saw two openings one day for a field director and an executive director of a pro-life organization I had never heard about, Students for Life of America. I immediately applied for the field director position and was soon contacted for an interview.

During the interview, I was told that I was being considered for the executive director position. I loved the ideas the board members of the organization were talking to me about—a chance to help other students like me start and grow their pro-life groups on campuses and to show them that they weren't alone in their convictions. It was a chance of a lifetime to help expand the pro-life movement and raise up a new generation of leaders, something that no one had ever tried before. I was sold on the vision.

To this day, I still don't know what caused me to accept the position. My only thought is that it has to have been the Holy Spirit

guiding me. I was leaving my comfortable, secure, well-paying government job to start a non-profit with no experience, no office, and no
staff. However, I was encouraged by the fact that SFLA had something
most non-profits never have: a grant from a very generous foundation
that ensured I would have a salary and could fund the organization
for three years. It was an opportunity and the risk of a lifetime.

At the time, I had never thought about myself as an entrepre-
neur, but that is what I was about to become. I was taking a huge
risk, taking a vision and turning it into a mission and systems for
success. The credit all goes to my husband, Jonathan, for not dis-
couraging me from the crazy idea at the time and for putting up
with the seventy-hour work weeks and weekends away since then.

Nine years later, SFLA is the largest pro-life youth organization
in America. Our demand is exceeding our capacity with staff and
funding; it's at an all-time high. We currently work with over 900
groups across the nation. Our once-simple mission of starting and
growing college pro-life groups and organizing a national conference
of 450 students has grown to include high schools, homeschools, law
and medical schools, and two sold-out national conferences of 2,700
young people. Our programs have expanded into more than ten
different training programs, more than fifteen regional conferences
per year, a group auditing program that awards thousands of dollars
in prizes and cash to groups every year, various printed educational
materials and postcards, "Events in a Box" ideas, comprehensive
training websites, leadership fellowship programs, and a Pregnant
on Campus initiative to help groups provide tangible resources and
support to pregnant and parenting women and men on campus.

Every program and resource we develop and provide free of
charge to student groups starts with one question: what would I
have liked to have when I was a pro-life student? Every program
and resource we develop starts with one vision: this is the generation with the greatest chance to abolish legal abortion, but we must
train them first.

The longer I have been working for Students for Life, the more I have become convinced of our vision and the possibility of achieving that vision. Every day the students we train do heroic things on their campuses—without being asked or paid and without hoping for media attention. They do them simply to try to save women and children from what our society and their parent's generation have mislabeled "choice."

Having the opportunity to help co-found and organize national coalition efforts like the De-Fund Planned Parenthood, Stop the Abortion Mandate, and Healthcare for Gunner coalitions has given SFLA and me an opportunity to lead and change the national debate about abortion in a way I never thought would be possible. I have had the privilege to take the devastating blow of my first son's diagnosis of cystic fibrosis and educate the nation about healthcare rationing. I've worked to mobilize other mothers and fathers of children with incurable diseases and physical battles that we know are not only targeted for abortion in utero, but are also being "rationed out" of the national healthcare system. Instead of feeling helpless and overcome by the burden of the loss of 3,300 preborn children a day, and by my son's devastating diagnosis, my position within the pro-life movement has allowed me to motivate and mobilize others, and to give a voice to those who aren't being heard.

I am witnessing the end of legal abortion. Our culture is changing, this generation of young people is becoming more pro-life, and the abortion industry admits that it is fighting a severe loss of intensity among its youth, an aging leadership, and technology which proves that abortion destroys a human life.

More work must be done. I try to remind people that our movement is similar to the abolitionist movement. It's not a quick fight but a long battle that will be victorious. But during the entire battle, we constantly have to paint the picture of how our nation will be able to survive without the injustice of abortion.

Despite the huge obstacles we have faced in Washington, D.C., I think we can see from the victories the pro-life movement has achieved in recent years that the abolition of abortion in our lifetime can actually happen. Think about a society in which all life is treated as a precious gift, a society in which women and families in crisis can turn to pregnancy help centers and their church family for support. Is it possible that the day will come when our political leaders respect life, when adoption is rightly understood as a positive and brave option, when birth mothers are celebrated, and when no woman ever feels forced to choose abortion for the sake of her education, career, or family? Envision a nation in which every woman facing an unplanned crisis pregnancy knows there is a place she can turn to for compassionate help.

Since that very first day at AIM Pregnancy Help Center, I have always known that I have wanted to fight in the pro-life movement. It's who I am. I know an injustice is happening daily, and I believe that as a Christian and as a human being, I am called to this work. Even the way God made me—bossy, competitive, type A, and loud-mouthed—is an obvious confirmation that he had a place for me in this movement. In fact, he has called my entire family into this work as my husband, Jonathan, and our sons, Gunner, Bear, and Maverick, often make sacrifices for Students for Life of America.

Being "pro-life" is not simply a job or something I do Monday through Friday; it's the way I live my life. Turning off being pro-life is not an option for me. I realize, ultimately, this is all God's work. He is the Author of life and I am excited about all that he is going to do through the pro-life movement in the future!

12

~

Conceived in Incest but Created by God: An Answer to the "Rape and Incest" Argument

Kristi Hofferber

In May of 1978, I was given up for adoption when I was only three days young. My adoptive parents were unable to have any children of their own, and were ecstatic that their dream of raising a child was about to come true. God placed me in the arms of two very loving people who took me in and provided me with unconditional love, support, and opportunities that shaped the foundation of the person that I am today.

I was raised in a Christian home and attended a Christian school up through fourth grade, which set the foundation of my faith. Although I remained active in the youth group at church, I still struggled through school, both socially and emotionally. I was not a social butterfly, did not make friends easily, and often enjoyed having time to myself. This pattern would continue through high school and into college. I had a few close friends, but even that too was difficult. If I began to feel like I was being left out, as I often did, it would put me into a state of depression and panic. I knew deep down what the real issue was, but I did not want to admit it even to myself. I did not know how to handle the fact that I was adopted. I did not know anyone else who was adopted that I could turn to for advice, and going to the psychologist for my behavioral outbursts with my family did not seem to be much help either. I could not open up to anyone, let alone find someone who understood my frustrations.

For as long as I can remember, my parents have been open with me about being adopted. It was not something that I needed to be ashamed of, but in a way, I still was. I was not ashamed of being adopted, I was ashamed of the way it made me feel—always angry and feeling like I did not belong in this world. As a matter of fact, I would often ask God, "Why am I here?" and "Why do I have to feel like this?" My high school years were the toughest years of my life. I would cry myself to sleep almost every night, praying to God to take away the pain in my heart.

Thank God that I had my faith to turn to, because I felt that I had nothing else. It was only when I was at church that I felt any semblance of peace. Something told me that I belonged there. One particular person at church made an impression on me that will last throughout my life. She is someone I will always look up to. She was my first grade teacher, and she was the one person in this world that I wanted to ask for help and guidance. If only I had had the confidence then. I now interact with her often. My husband is a minister, and has been called to the same church where I grew up. God is a marvelous God!

My husband is another special person God has brought into my life. He and I have been married almost ten years and have one son. The three of us share something very special as a family: we were all adopted. We are a family stitched together with God's love, and that was God's plan from the very beginning.

In April of 2008, I made the decision that the time had come for me to know exactly where I came from. I would be turning thirty in a little over a month and I realized that I had dreams that were not fulfilled. The "what ifs" were weighing heavily on my mind, as well as many other unanswered questions. There was never a day in my life that went by without me thinking "Is that person related to me?" wherever I went.

After a few weeks filled with anxiety and hesitation, I brought myself to ask my mom and dad for my background information. My adoptive mother almost sounded relieved that I had finally asked. She and my adoptive father were very honest with me. What I was about to find out was something that had never, in a million years, crossed my mind. After knowing only that my biological mother was sixteen when she gave birth to me, I found out that she was also a victim of incest and rape by her father, and that I was likely the result of these actions.

I was speechless! It took all I had to keep my composure. I went from having about a dozen questions in my mind, to having hundreds. The first question that I remember asking was "How would you know that if my adoption records were sealed?" Ironically, my adoptive mother worked at the hospital where I was born. She is unable to remember exactly how she had learned my birth mother's name, but having her name was also how she knew about the possible situation with my biological father. The truth about his past was published in 1991 when my biological mother prosecuted her father for not only the pregnancy that resulted in my birth and adoption, but also for six other pregnancies that resulted in five abortions and one miscarriage, all of which were forced by her father. Words could not begin to describe the emotions going on inside my mind at that moment. What kind of monster would do such a thing to his own daughter? Another question going through my mind was this: Given the fate of the other six children, why was I spared? Why wasn't I aborted also?

I thank God for showing me where to turn in times of crisis because this question could only be answered through Scripture. Romans 9:20 states, "But who are you, O man, to answer back to God? Will what is molded say to its molder, 'Why have you made me like this?'" (ESV). I do not need to ask why, because I already know why I survived. I was created intentionally by God for his purpose. He chose me! At the same time, my heart ached for the children just like me whose lives have been ended by abortion. They were formed by God just like me, regardless of how they were conceived. And I had even more concern for the true survivor, my biological mother. How could one person be put through such trauma? I was amazed at her fortitude despite so many years of abuse.

I thank God that my faith was strong at the time that I asked to know about my adoption. If my relationship with Christ had not been as mature, my view might have been very different. This just reinforces the fact that God's timing is perfect!

I really stewed on the information I received for about a week, praying and asking God to guide me to do his will. I felt that I was being guided to continue my search for my biological mother and the truth of my existence. I also wanted to consult with my husband before continuing with my search. It did take me a few days to tell him what I had found out. I did not fear his reaction, but at the time I was not even sure of my own reaction. After I shared the information with him, he expressed support for me by agreeing I should continue my search if that was what I felt led to do. I could not have asked for a better man by my side.

After only two short days of searching the internet, I came across a popular website that reunites schoolmates. It was here that I found a photo of my biological mother with an email address at the bottom. I had so many emotions and confusing thoughts going on in my head that I did not know exactly what to do; the moment that I had imagined for so long was no longer just a dream, it was finally a reality! When I found the courage to contact her, she soon responded and wanted me to call her right away. I can still remember the feeling I had in my stomach. It was like having a hundred butterflies fluttering around uncontrollably. I called her and when she answered the phone, I could tell she was nervous. I'm sure she could tell I was nervous, too. After about five minutes of conversation, the awkwardness left and it was smooth sailing. She and I spoke on the phone for well over an hour about some of the family's history and my upbringing.

After our initial conversation, we both agreed that we wanted to meet, along with her younger daughter, my half-sister, who I found out was expecting a child in just a few days. My half-sister was very excited and asked if I would like to visit when she had the baby. I was thrilled. I made quick arrangements to drive there over the coming weekend and we were all very excited. That same evening that we had talked, my half-sister had her baby. What a day to remember! Three days later, I was on the road to visit. I decided it was a trip that I would take alone, even though my parents were concerned about me driving by myself. I knew that God would guide me and protect me.

The drive only took about six hours, which went very quickly. We all met for breakfast, including my new nephew. I could not believe that the day I had thought about for so long was finally here! We talked briefly at breakfast and spent the morning together looking at pictures and getting to know each other. I was literally in awe at the resemblance between my biological mother and me. Later that afternoon, my biological mother sat with me on a bench near a beautiful lake just talking about everything. It was also at this time that she felt comfortable enough to tell me about my biological father. As she began to explain, I let her know that I already had an idea who my biological father was. This was also when I let her know about my faith and how I felt about who I was. "My father may share my DNA, but God created me. No matter the circumstance, it is of God's will and purpose that I was conceived."

It is very hard for me to describe my feelings toward my biological father. The sinner in me wants to see him punished for his actions, considering he only served less than eighteen months in prison due to lack of evidence—me. However, my Christian upbringing taught me to be different. After all, I would not be here if it were not for his actions, and I am thankful to be here. But don't get me wrong—I absolutely do not approve of what he did.

I was later granted the opportunity to speak to my biological father, and I simply asked him if he had asked for forgiveness. His reply was yes, and he also apologized to my biological mother at that time. It is my prayer that he had truly asked God for forgiveness, because he passed away in the fall of 2011. It was a most difficult encounter, but I am glad I had that conversation.

The reality of it all hit me during the second day of my visit with my mother. I woke up early in the morning and sat on the porch for several hours by myself, crying profusely. No matter how hard I tried, I just could not stop. It was twenty-nine years of bottled emotions that were pouring out. All I could do besides cry at this point was offer prayers of thanksgiving that I finally got to meet the person who gave birth to me. It was truly a miracle!

That evening, we drove about an hour to visit with my biological mother's brother and his family. This was something that meant a lot to my biological mother. Growing up, her brother did not believe that the events that took place between my biological mother and father had really happened, as his father wanted him to think they did not. Finally showing her brother that there was truth to her claims was a form of closure for her. For her brother, it was a shock! He now believed her after all this time and it felt good for me to know that the truth finally brought them closer again.

A few short weeks after my first visit with my biological family, my biological mother came to visit me and my family. I was able to introduce her to my adoptive parents and many of my close friends. Although this was a bit awkward for all of us, it was one of the most precious moments in my life! I also got to meet some of my biological mother's family who still lived within forty miles of where I live now. It really is a small world! Her family here was also happy that the truth was finally revealed and the family had been brought together again. My hope is that the family that was torn apart by secrets and lies and has now been brought together can begin to be healed by the truth. There is no doubt in my mind that God was in control of it all. There is no other explanation! I was finally beginning to see the pieces of my life fitting together. He turned my feelings of being broken and unworthy to that of having unending value. Through Christ I have gained the confidence necessary to fulfill my dreams after having searched for so long on my own. I am not defined by my DNA, but by the calling I have received as a child of God. No one can take that away from me. My calling in Christ Jesus is my destiny! He is my foundation, and with him I cannot crumble.

I learned something very important during this time in my life. Life is about the faith that we have in Christ, the hope only he can give us for tomorrow, and spreading his love to everyone around us! I was even given the opportunity to share my faith with someone who has had many obstacles to overcome in life, and help her to move on.

I say this to anyone who discovers they are the result of rape or incest: look to Christ for strength in everything! Even in these terrible cases of rape and incest, each preborn child is created by God for a purpose! The Scripture says, "As for you, you meant evil against me, but God meant it for good" (Gen 50:20 ESV). My life is now a testimony of something good: God can take the actions of evil and make them an opportunity to do something miraculous!

13

~

Abortion Survivor

Melissa Ohden

Abortion is a decision that has such a detrimental effect on so many, across generations. Sadly, we know that there is often little choice behind that decision, whether lack of knowledge about resources and support, coercion, and even force are the impetus for it. Little did anyone realize when my own biological mother was forced to undergo a saline infusion abortion at St. Luke's Hospital in Sioux City, Iowa, in 1977, that this one decision, this one moment in time, would have such far-reaching effects on so many people's lives.

On August 24, 1977, a nineteen-year-old college student who was pregnant with her boyfriend's child was forced to undergo a saline infusion abortion. She believed she was around five months pregnant. A syringe full of a toxic salt solution was injected into the amniotic fluid surrounding her rapidly developing child in the womb. Over the next few days, the baby was subjected to that toxic salt solution, and just as sadly, that woman was subjected to the painful process of her pregnancy being ended as her child's life was being snuffed out, her child's tiny body convulsing in the womb as the child was scalded to death. "Candy apple babies," the children who are aborted by saline are often called, their bodies blackened by the saline solution before it reaches their internal organs.

The mother returns later in the week with the intent of delivering her baby, her dead baby, through a labor induction. As the pitocin drip opens her womb, the closed, darkened tomb of her child is prematurely opened. Her perfectly formed daughter with dark hair and delicate features is delivered. It is done. She will be "taken care of" later, discarded like medical waste. But she's a child! A perfectly formed child. Yet, this is her fate, to be entombed in her mother's womb, and after being forcefully removed, to be laid to rest for all eternity in the trash. Nameless, faceless, and voiceless, she was someone's daughter. She was someone's granddaughter. She was someone's niece, someone's sister. But they will never know. They will never know that she existed. They will never know how her short life was extinguished in the very place she felt safe and protected. They will never know.

For now, she's simply moved aside, out of the way of the nurse tending to the young woman, out of the eyesight of the mother who has been going through the process of her daughter's death, a process that has been going on inside her now for days. It is done.

But God creates beauty from ashes. He breathes life into those who are lifeless. He brings the truth out of the darkness and into the light. And by his grace, as the baby girl he created was so brazenly attacked and left for dead in a coldly clinical hospital room, he gave her the strength to move the tiny limbs of her two-pound-fourteen-ounce body and gasp for breath with her tiny mouth. And by all accounts that I've heard, this was when the nursing staff realized that this precious baby girl had been unsuccessfully aborted, that she was born alive, and the process of life-sustaining medical care began.

Of course, by now, I'm sure you can guess that the baby girl assaulted with the toxic salt solution in the womb and left to be disposed of was me. It's awe-inspiring for me to be able to share about my sufferings at the hands of an abortionist. But it is even more awe-inspiring to share about how the Lord had his hand on me in my birth mother's womb, protecting me from certain death.

I will likely never know all that led up to my biological mother entering the hospital that day, having been forced to end my life. But what I do know motivates me to tell my story and the stories of both of my biological parents and their families, with the hopes that lives like mine will be saved, lives like theirs will be transformed, and generations will be saved and healed from the pain of abortion.

Although it was believed that my biological mother was less than five months pregnant with me, the fact that I weighed almost three pounds and that I survived outside the womb points to the fact that she was much farther along in her pregnancy than they realized. The medical records that I finally received in 2007 regarding my birth confirm this. These records clearly discuss the abortion with statements such as "a saline infusion for an abortion was done but was unsuccessful." And one of the first notations by a doctor indicates that I looked like I was approximately thirty-one weeks' gestational age when I was aborted unsuccessfully. Yet whether my biological mother was thirty-one weeks or thirty-one days pregnant, the outcome was meant to be the same: I was intended to die from an abortion.

When you think of an abortion survivor, what comes to mind? Children scalded to death? Torn apart? Left to die if they do survive? I had never even encountered the reality of children surviving abortions when I found out the truth about my life at the age of fourteen, but I knew that I'm not what most people have in mind. In fact, if you passed me on the street today, you would never guess that I survived the abortion procedure and that, having survived, I had to fight for my life once again. Because of what the toxic salt solution was starting to do to my body, I required multiple blood transfusions. I suffered from severe respiratory and liver problems and seizures, and the prognosis for my life was poor indeed. The doctors made it clear that they didn't expect for me to live for very long, and if I did survive, I would have multiple disabilities ranging from being blind and deaf to having emotional and mental disabilities.

Yet survive I did; and, dare I say, I've thrived. After the failed abortion attempt, an adoption plan was made for me. I am forever grateful to my birth parents for ultimately giving me life, no matter what attempts others made to end it. I'm equally grateful for the gift of my adoptive family. My adoptive parents first met me when I was still in the Neo-Natal Intensive Care Unit (NICU) in Iowa City, Iowa, where I was transferred from St. Luke's not long after I was born. Despite the poor prognosis that the doctors had for my life, my adoptive parents didn't hesitate for a second to open their hearts and their home to me. They openly share in radio and television interviews that the first time that they laid eyes on me as I lay in the incubator, full of tubes and wires, they fell in love with me.

I was blessed to go home to my adoptive family within just two months of surviving the failed abortion. I know that it was the love of my adoptive parents and the nurses and doctors who cared for me that helped me not only to survive, but to thrive. Over the years, I have been blessed to meet a number of the nurses and volunteers who cared for me during my time in the NICU. I know that it wasn't just great medical care that allowed me to go home to my family within such a short period of time; it was the great care and the great love I received. The individuals who cared for me nurtured me, believed in me, gave me a name when I was nameless, and loved me that I might have life. I am forever grateful to all these ordinary men and women who gave me extraordinary love and care. I believe they each played an important part in making me the woman that I am today. For despite the initial concerns regarding my life, I am a healthy woman in her mid-thirties, a wife and mother who is free from any long-lasting consequences of the abortion procedure meant to end her life and her subsequent premature birth.

My journey to this point in my life and the amazing blessings that I've received over the years could fill this entire book! My life has been full of poignant moments, amazing experiences that have shown me not only how blessed I am to be alive and to have been given the opportunity to be a voice for the millions of children who have been rendered voiceless from abortion, but also to show how far-reaching the impact of abortion truly is.

On April 26, 2008, a beautiful girl, Olivia Eva Sophia Ohden, was born at St. Luke's Hospital in Sioux City, Iowa. Yes, thirty-one years after I was aborted and left to die at St. Luke's Hospital, our oldest daughter was born at the very same place! It's an amazing story, indeed. I even ended up moving to Sioux City as an adult to finish my master's degree in social work, knowing that it was in this city, in that hospital, that my life was supposed to end. But it's much more amazing to learn what happened when our daughter was born at that hospital. The very place that once brought me great fear and anxiety has now been transformed into holding the most beautiful memories of my life. I hope that by reading my experience you will be encouraged to see that there is nothing in this world that can't be redeemed, no circumstance that can't be changed, nothing too difficult for God. Indeed, beauty can come from ashes.

Late in the winter of 2008, Ryan and I attended our birthing class at St. Luke's on a cold, snowy Saturday morning. We were painfully aware that we were attempting to change the course of its history. We could have chosen to attend a class at the other hospital in town, but we wanted to see if we, and especially I, could withstand being at the hospital for the class. If so, then maybe we would be able give birth there, because this hospital is renowned for its obstetric care. We waited almost two hours for the class to start, with no instructor in sight. My fears about the hospital's past came creeping in. I was ready to run (at that point in my pregnancy it was more like a waddle!) away from it all, when the instructor finally arrived and the class began.

"My name is Lori, and I've worked here since the mid-1970s," the nurse instructor told the class. *The mid-1970s?!* A silent alarm was ringing in my head. I knew she had to know about me and my survival. Later that morning, I rather boldly walked up to her and introduced myself. "I think you might know me," I stated. "I survived a failed abortion attempt here back in 1977." "Of course I know who you are," Lori quickly replied, huge tears streaming down her face. "You look just like your grandmother." I don't know what was more shocking to me, the fact that she indeed knew and remembered me, or that she said that I looked like my maternal grandmother, whom I knew had been a nurse educator at the time that I survived.

A few short paragraphs can't do justice to that whole experience, but I hope that you can gather that it changed my life and set the course for our daughter's life. And it wasn't long after Olivia's arrival that my ten-year-long search brought me into contact with some members of my biological family. Although I never met my biological father, who passed away in 2008 just months after I contacted him, through his passing, he gave me the great gift of his family. When he passed away, they discovered the letter that I had sent him months previously and they learned of the great secret my father had kept throughout his life and carried to his grave: the abortion in 1977 and his child who survived. Olivia was just six weeks old the first time that I met my paternal grandfather, Don. My grandfather and my great aunt, Vicki, are two of my favorite people in this world, and we are blessed to have them in our lives.

Despite not yet having the chance to meet my biological parents, or the majority of my biological family, I see abortion through the lens of each of our lives. I have seen how my biological mother's forced abortion didn't just affect my life and hers, it's affected all of our lives. Secrets have been kept, relationships have been changed. Some relationships have ended. Shame, guilt, and resentment have abounded in our lives. And I live each day of my life knowing that if the abortion had succeeded in ending my life, my two daughters never would have existed. This is the most difficult part of it all for me. Every decision has a consequence; every abortion has a ripple effect that impacts generations. That is the biggest reason why I came forward publicly in 2007 as an abortion survivor, to turn back the tide in the opposite direction, to bring truth and love to a world that has been devastated by abortion.

Lives like mine, stories like mine, are often unheard of in a world where abortion is still talked about as a simple choice or a woman's right. Thankfully, however, the truth about abortion and its consequences for children, women, men, families, and our communities as a whole is coming to light. The truth about abortion survivors is that I'm far from alone. Although we mourn the loss of nearly 57 million lives to abortion in the years since *Roe v. Wade* was passed, we also celebrate the lives of those who have survived.

And there certainly are other survivors! In 2012, I launched the Abortion Survivors Network, which seeks to educate the public about abortion and survivors, while simultaneously providing a network of support to survivors. As I was researching articles to include on the website, I learned that there are an estimated 44,000 abortion survivors in the U.S. alone (possibly more)! These figures are based on failure rates of late term abortions as reported by the Center for Disease Control (CDC).

I want to find and connect with those 44,000 survivors. I have a long way to go, having currently heard from just under 200 others like me, but I'm off to a good start. Every week I hear from at least one new survivor. I often hear from many more. As a survivor who felt so alone for so many years, it brings me great joy to hear how finding this network and connecting with other survivors is now changing the lives of other abortion survivors. Looking back on my life, the lives of my family members, and our world, I know that abortion has forever changed the landscape of our culture, but I don't despair. There have been countless lives spared, there has been healing brought to countless lives, there have been countless individuals converted, and the rise in the pro-life movement continues.

14

Adoptees United for Life

Jim and Wendy Sable

Wendy: I always knew I was adopted. As a young girl I used to wonder about the "other woman" who gave birth to me and gave me to my mom and dad to be their daughter. As I got older and understood reproduction and genetics, the questions in my head about "her" multiplied. What did she look like? Was her vision as bad as mine? Did she have red curly hair like me? Was she a lefty too? Did she love to sing? I somehow instinctively knew that I needed to thank her for not having an abortion. I do not remember a birthday ever passing without thinking about her, and wondering if she remembered me too.

Jim: How many people really think about their conception? I think contemplating one's own conception elicits a response of "too much information." But I think about it every day because I was conceived in rape. At first, the daily thoughts were anguish-filled and suffocating. Being adopted, I was told I was born to an unwed mother. Even though she surrendered me, I hoped I had been formed from an act of love. I created two special people in my imagination who, despite their love, found themselves in a difficult situation, faced with a tough decision. I even accepted the possibility that their love only lasted briefly. I hoped that my conception had at least occurred from a positive moment between my biological parents.

Wendy: On the night Neil Armstrong walked on the moon, two teenagers in Nashville, Tennessee, "celebrated" the historic event. I was born eight months later in March, 1970 and was placed for adoption through Catholic Charities at five weeks old. My mom and dad raised me and my two adopted sisters in a northwestern suburb of Chicago. I had an amazing childhood with loving and giving parents who provided me with all I needed. I always knew I was adopted, but it was not a topic of conversation, as my parents never wanted me or my sisters to be treated any differently than other "biological" children.

Jim: Walking home from work one night, a thirty-five-year-old woman was attacked and raped. She became pregnant with me from this rape. I was born just over seven months later, in April of 1958. I was adopted through Catholic Charities and placed at five months old, a little older than the typical adoption. My mom and dad raised me and my adopted sister in the same northwestern suburb where Wendy lived. I had a wonderful childhood. My parents were very loving and we lived in a supportive neighborhood that included other families with adopted children.

Wendy: Anxious about a developing medical issue at age twenty-four, I initially contacted Catholic Charities to get non-identifying medical information. I needed to find out if there was anything genetically related in my records. A letter arrived with the requested information, but it also unexpectedly informed me that my birth mother kept her contact information available for me, should I ever want to find her. She had married, but kept her maiden name to make it easier for me to find her. There were letters and pictures in my folder from her as well. Wow! I hemmed and hawed over opening that Pandora's box. After much contemplation, I decided to pursue contacting her. Three months later, Catholic Charities facilitated our reunion.

Jim: At forty-seven, my curiosity conquered my caution, so I petitioned Catholic Charities for non-identifying information. The letter arrived and stated that my biological mother was "assaulted" and I was conceived from that "assault." I sat in stunned silence, shocked to receive every adopted child's nightmare in that envelope. I shut down. It took two years of working with a therapist and the support of my wife to get over the stigma of being a "rape baby." Finally, with the help of a dear friend, we searched for my birth mother based on the limited information I had. I wanted answers. We discovered my birth mother had passed away just over a year prior, but found that my birth mother's sister was living about half an hour away from us. I nervously wrote a letter to this sister, hoping our search located the right person. Forty-eight hours later the phone rang. I heard a kind voice say, "This story sounds very familiar," and she acknowledged that I was, indeed, her nephew. We shared a long conversation on the phone, and a meeting was quickly arranged.

Wendy: My birth mother's family moved from Chicago to Nashville when she was in high school. She developed a relationship with a schoolmate, and at sixteen she had to tell her parents she was pregnant. Immediately, both sets of parents separated the two.

Determined to get rid of "the problem," her father took her twice for an illegal abortion, but she "chickened out." Then her father forced it a third time. Defeated, she got up on the table, but as the procedure was about to start, she kicked the abortionist, got off the table, and ran out. Her father then ordered her older brother to beat her so she would miscarry. The brother was unable to harm his sister and did not follow through. Still desperate to get rid of "the problem," her father forced her to drink quinine to force a miscarriage, but the miscarriage never came. So she was sent to Catholic Charities' St. Vincent's Mother and Baby Shelter in Chicago, where she spent almost six months.

She claimed that her treatment at St. Vincent's was abusive and demeaning. She never could share the details with me, other than that their treatment turned her away from the Catholic Church. She went into labor on Palm Sunday and I was born at St. Joseph's Hospital weighing just over six pounds. Five days later, she signed the release papers and left for Texas to live with her oldest sister until the school year finished. She sent one letter to my biological father stating that I was born and that I had been placed for adoption. She never knew if he received it.

Her truth and the struggle of her story was a lot for me to process. Somehow I never felt angry at her father, understanding the times (1969), and that he was a proud man with a limited education trying to save the honor of his family. I actually met him the same day I met her. I was never spoken of until I made contact. That day an old, gentle man held me in his arms, crying, and could not let go of his granddaughter. Forgiveness was easy. He was my grandpa until he died, and I loved him.

Jim: Meeting with my aunt was bittersweet, as she was my only connection to answer all the questions I had about my birth mother and my past. My aunt described my birth mother as a reserved and quiet woman, devout in her faith and with a steady moral compass. Her story was that while walking home from work she had been attacked and raped by an unknown man. She said nothing about the rape, but went into a frozen emotional shutdown. She did not say anything about the pregnancy. She showed minimally and even near the end of her pregnancy she referred to her baby bump as a "tumor." Her silence and her actions all speak of a deep, acute trauma.

Two weeks before I was born, she finally told her parents. This thirty-five-year-old woman's parents jumped into action and took her to Catholic Charities' St. Vincent's Mother and Baby Shelter in Chicago. She went into premature labor on the day she was to be admitted and I was born at Lewis Memorial Hospital at about seven and a half month's gestation, weighing just over five pounds. I was held back from being adopted due to "the nature of my conception" to make sure I was healthy. After I was relinquished, I was never discussed again. My birth mother married in 1959, but never had other children. As the years went by and her life waned, her decision not to speak to anyone about being raped never changed, even at the very last moments of her life.

Wendy: For my thirtieth birthday, my birth mother found my biological father in Chattanooga, Tennessee. He was married and had three sons. She contacted him first and gave me his email address. My first note to him was timid, expressing my desire not to disturb his life, to respect his privacy and, if this was the only contact we had, that I could accept his decision. The return email was loving and welcoming—his wife knew he had a daughter and, surprisingly, the three boys knew they had a half-sister. A flurry of emails was exchanged and we talked on the phone.

Within weeks, my birth father, his wife, and his youngest son made the trip to Chicago for a reunion. My birth mother joined us—it was the first time they had seen each other since they announced she was pregnant. It was a very emotional day for all of us . . . a miracle really, to have the two people who created me in one room. Pictures were taken—the only pictures I have of me with both my biological parents. My birth father gave me a small envelope and the contents spoke volumes about his character. Enclosed, among other things, was a letter that an eighteen-year-old boy received thirty years earlier—my one and only birth announcement. It was the letter my birth mother sent him after giving me up. He held onto it for thirty years, never forgetting or denying that he had a daughter. I still stay in touch with my birth father, but my relationship with my birth mother became complicated and separation from her was necessary. Among other issues that divided us, I was most saddened by her immovable pro-choice position.

Jim: After I cultivated a friendship with my aunt, she wanted me to meet her six children. My cousins never knew their aunt (my birth mother) had a baby and were shocked by the news just a year after her death. Shock quickly faded to acceptance and welcome, and we met on a few occasions. My cousins were very curious about this newly found relative and my resemblance to a few of them was undeniable. We have stayed in touch.

The time finally came for my last step, to visit my mother's grave. I am still not sure why I postponed going, other than just waiting to be completely emotionally ready. Once there, I sat on the ground next to her grave for some time and prayed. I knew I was with her spirit. I cleaned off her headstone and cemented a golden pin with two little baby feet into the rosary cut into the granite to honor our brief time together. I wanted her to know her son was there, and that he loved her and was so thankful for her courage.

I used to shy away from the rape exception. The furthest I would go would be to say—"The rape exception is wrong. In a perfect world there would be no rape, but I do not want to be the one to tell that woman she has to endure the pregnancy." Now, I have heard many stories about how giving birth after a rape conception can be healing. I hope my birth mother found some healing in giving me life.

Wendy: I met Jim twenty-four years ago through a mutual friend who mentioned he also had an adopted friend. We were setting Jim up on a blind date with my girlfriend. I knew within five minutes of meeting him I was dating the wrong guy. Over time, we developed a friendship and shared our adoption stories together, at least what we knew of them at that point. A unique bond formed from sharing such a common past—a bond that only another adopted person could understand. Time marched on as we dated other people, but God's will finally put us on the same track. We dated only three months before Jim proposed and I said yes, with all my heart!

Jim: When I first met Wendy, I felt an undeniable yet difficult-to-identify attraction and bond with her. Polar opposites in temperament, I didn't think my easy-going, shy personality could be compatible with the bubbly, energetic spirit of this young woman. It took a while for us to realize that we were meant to be together.

Friendship turned into dating, and then quickly grew into love. In no time at all, I realized she was "the one." Our relationship has undoubtedly been made stronger because of our shared adoption experiences. Wendy's support and our love for each other have provided a shelter during my stormy journey. With God's grace, our journey continues.

We have now been married for nineteen years, bonded by our incredible common adoptive past and amazing stories of how we even exist. How these two adoptees with such a common past were brought together had to be the will of God. We share our pro-life commitment with the fullest understanding that our very lives depended on the laws that protected us. If we had been conceived after 1973, we know it is very likely that neither of us would be here. However, we also know God brought us together because he had an amazing plan for us. We hope our story enlightens others.

Amazing good, love, and life can spring forth from tragic and difficult circumstances. We are blessed with three wonderful sons. We will always have eternal love and gratitude for our parents who loved and raised us, for two strong birth mothers who gave us the chance to live, and for one welcoming biological father.

We grieve deeply for every aborted baby. Before knowing our own stories, we used to be pro-life quietly, from a distance, only occasionally dipping our toes into the turbulent waters of the abortion debate. Now, we fearlessly dive into the roiling waves created by the legalization of abortion, and do so frequently and with great faith. We are unafraid to proclaim truth. We are honored and humbled to take part in Face the Truth Tours, organizations such as Save the 1 and Hope After Rape Conception, Planned Parenthood protests, clinic vigils, pregnancy support center activities, and other pro-life ministries.

We can proclaim without any hesitation or doubt—every life matters!

15

~

Abortion Abolitionist: The Story of a Selfless Servant, Kortney Blythe Gordon

Told by her father, Larry Blythe

"How can we expect righteousness to prevail when there is hardly anyone willing to give himself up individually to a righteous cause? Such a fine, sunny day, and I have to go, but what does my death matter, if through us thousands of people are awakened and stirred to action?"—Sophie Scholl

Bowing her head to pray for the end of abortion in front of the U.S. Supreme Court, Kortney Blythe Gordon would read the words "to live is Christ, to die is gain" tattooed on her feet. So great was her commitment to save the lives of these tiny humans being led to slaughter that she labeled herself with the fitting title, "abortion abolitionist." Her prayers and activism were repeated hundreds, perhaps thousands of times at abortion clinics, schools, universities, protests, and marches. This tireless, passionate, pro-life hero rocked the world, accomplishing more for God in twenty-eight years than many Christians do in their entire lives. Kortney saved countless preborn children from death, shared the gospel of Jesus Christ, and tremendously impacted the lives of thousands of others through training, teaching, and one-on-one discipleship. I am amazed, blessed, and grateful that God permitted me to be her father. She was a solid woman of God with a faith, love, and zeal we should long for as believers.

From childhood Kortney had a unique love for God and others. She was a child after God's own heart. Her keen intelligence and sensitivity to spiritual things were initially developed through her adolescent and teen years but were always increasing.

Kortney trusted Jesus as her Savior at a very young age. As the daughter of a youth pastor and Christian apologist, Kortney was exposed to many church events, mission trips, and discussions about theology and defending the truth of the Christian faith. I believe this laid the foundation which led to her amazing effectiveness as a defender of the preborn.

As Kortney grew in the Lord, her bold passion for Christ and the gospel became more evident and she would proclaim the truth to anyone and everyone. She was inspired, thrilled, and overjoyed at seeing many babies saved through the ministry of At The Well Ministries, founded by her Uncle Don. This ministry has saved well over 3,500 preborn children from being led to the slaughter. Kortney's desire to be a pediatrician was soon replaced by an intense zeal and consuming desire to "do what Uncle Don does"—saving preborn humans from the grasp of abortion centers. She would later in life develop her own personal mission statement: "Jesus Christ is my Lord, abolishing abortion is my calling." As history will record, she lived this mission to the fullest.

Kortney attended her first "Life Chain," a great pro-life community outreach developed by abolitionist Royce Dunn, when she was about six years old. She was thrilled to stand along the streets with many other Christians proclaiming the gospel and pleading with passersby to be pro-life. But it was seeing the pictures of real saved babies and the stories Uncle Don told about precious lives saved that solidified the decision in her heart to pursue this calling. As we would visit some of the "killing centers" where Uncle Don did his sidewalk counseling, Kortney would be in awe at hearing her uncle encourage moms to come and talk with him as he would share "a better answer to their problem." Then he would share the gospel of the death, burial, and resurrection of Jesus and how they could place their trust in him alone. Many were saved both spiritually and physically, including clinic workers, security guards, and clinic escorts.

After excelling in elementary, junior high, and high school, Kortney attended Montreat College in North Carolina. She continued to grow in the Lord, developed exceptional writing skills, and eventually became the editor of the college newspaper, *The Whetstone*, from 2002 to 2005. She also worked in the writing center helping students write better reports. She had a gift for writing and for counseling people one-on-one. Although Kortney was raised by a Christian apologist-debater, she developed her own unique way of toning down the conversation just enough to be firm in her convictions, powerful in her arguments, and competent in intellectual prowess. Kortney had the ability to effectively draw her opponents into a respectful relationship in which they would actually listen to her and be swayed. In 2005 she graduated magna cum laude from Montreat College with a bachelor of arts degree in English, with a focus on communication.

Kortney began to aggressively develop her pro-life ministry throughout her college years by doing sidewalk counseling at abortion clinics, attending marches, protests, and driving hours to youth events and music festivals. Kortney loved Rock for Life and would later work for them full time. RFL was started by Bryan Kemper and Erik Whittington. Erik was initially motivated into action after observing a "life chain" and seeing a sign that read simply "Abortion Kills Children." Rock for Life later moved from Oregon to Virginia and joined forces with American Life League. Their original purpose was to reach youth with the pro-life message through large rock music concerts. Much of this was done at the annual Christian rock festival Cornerstone, which would draw tens of thousands of people. The Rock for Life tent or booth would provide literature, seminars, and bold pro-life volunteers to speak the truth about abortion and answer objections from pro-abortion advocates and "on-the-fence" pro-lifers. Erik Whittington of Rock for Life would later recount his first introduction to Kortney:

> Kortney was a tireless advocate for the preborn. She was extremely intelligent, a great communicator and organizer . . . Kortney was friendly, loved our Lord, and didn't have a mean bone in her body. She always had a smile on her face and a kind word to say.[1]

An activist was born—or nurtured. Kortney continued to develop her skills in speaking the truth about abortion, the gospel, theology, and Christian apologetics. Although she was not formally trained in philosophy she grew mightily in intellect gained from reading literature and the Bible, and from our many discussions about answers to difficult questions, atheism, defending Christianity, and much more. I had to attend years of seminary to learn what Kortney learned from countless hours of discussion and reading. She became what a dad could only hope and pray for his daughter—a chaste woman of God and a highly effective Christian apologist, which gave her the fuel to be a mighty defender of life in the pro-life movement.

When Kortney graduated from college, she took her first paid pro-life job working as a night-time residential supervisor for the unwed mother's home Room at the Inn. Under the welcoming guidance and enthusiastic leadership of Cindy Brown, her boss, and Jeannie Wray, executive director, Kortney developed a love and appreciation for unwed mothers. She was a mentor to moms by night, pro-life activist on weekends, and a bank teller by day.

In the summer of 2006, Kortney was contacted by Jeff White, founder of the southern-California-based pro-life activist group Survivors of the Abortion Holocaust. Kortney joined the team as

Survivors' campus life tour director. During her three years with Survivors she trained many future pro-life leaders, and led many tours in California and across the country presenting the pro-life message at colleges, universities, and high schools. She was also able to spend several days in Australia training people and alerting them to disinformation from anti-life promoters and the devastating impact of abortion upon society.

Kortney, along with many other heroes, paved the way in many cities across America for others to fight for the civil rights of the preborn. She was arrested unjustly a total of nine times, and was exonerated a total of nine times. Never once did she break any laws. Kortney and her team had to stand firm and proclaim the anti-abortion message without compromise and without backing down. Their normal operation was to visit a public college or university, set up signs about freedom of speech on campuses, hand out literature, and speak with students in a calm, professional, and respectful manner. On high school campuses, Kortney and her team would do the same, but outside the schools on the public sidewalks, never entering the school property. Numerous times their free speech would be challenged and they would be asked to leave. Kortney would politely ask, "On what grounds?" The answer would usually be "trespassing," to which she would reply, "How can we trespass on public property?" Her team was professionally counseled and defended by the Life Legal Defense Foundation under the tremendous guidance of Katie Short, Allison Aranda, and others.

On one of their tours to the University of California, Berkeley, while they were politely and legally exercising their first amendment rights on a public campus, the board of regents warned Kortney, the Survivors team, and Uncle Don that they would all be arrested if they didn't leave immediately. In her professional, respectful manner Kortney asked, "What would you be arresting us for?" The regent replied "trespassing." Kortney responded that the free speech laws of the state could not be ignored or superseded by the board of regents and that they would continue lawfully speaking with students and handing out literature. Minutes later Kortney was arrested on that very spot. The Survivors sued the campus and city and won the lawsuit. Kortney and her team were exonerated and freedom of speech laws were enacted in the city as a result of *Blythe v. the City of Berkeley.*

Kortney led the Campus Life Tour of Survivors to Columbia College in the spring of 2007. Again she and her team were arrested and again they went to court. She and her team were unanimously acquitted of criminal charges of causing a campus disturbance. During the trial the judge declared the college's free speech policy unconstitutional because it required individuals to apply for a permit. The college community changed its policy and now welcomes free speech advocates rather than censoring them. Kortney and the team returned a year later and were greeted with open arms by the same college officials who had had them unlawfully arrested.

Another blatant violation of the first amendment happened in Birmingham, Alabama, in 2009. Kortney and eight other Survivors were peacefully handing out literature, holding signs, and speaking to students on the public sidewalk in front of a local high school. More than a dozen Birmingham police officers arrived and engaged in what the Life Legal Defense Foundation called "outrageous civil rights violations" against the nine, forcing them to spend fourteen hours in the same jail cell where Martin Luther King Jr. was jailed in 1963. Dr. King was arrested for taking part in the Birmingham campaign, a non-violent protest conducted by the Alabama Christian Movement for Human Rights. Now in 2009, history seemed to repeat itself. A police officer told one of Kortney's team members that the sidewalk was private, not public property for "non-citizens of Birmingham." The group politely refused to leave. They were arrested, and their video equipment and vehicle were confiscated. In the process the police damaged their van, destroyed some of the video evidence, and tried to have their hotel rooms searched.

During the arrests, Kortney repeatedly asked one of the officers the reason for the arrests. The officer kept assuring her that her team was not being arrested, but was only being detained and did not know on what basis they would be charged. The Survivors were never informed why they were being handcuffed and jailed. All nine Survivors were forced to wear orange jumpsuits, were placed in cells for six hours without access to water, phones, or bathrooms, and were ignored by their jailors. While in her cell, Kortney was questioned by an officer regarding their actions. Kortney told him that the Constitution of the United States protected their right to stand on the public sidewalk.

After their release the next morning, the rest of the team continued on tour while Kortney remained in Birmingham for a few days and scheduled a press conference demanding the return of the Survivors' four video cameras. As the press conference was about to begin, Kortney was contacted by one of the officers promising the release of their property. He apologized to Kortney and the return of the property was filmed by ABC News of Birmingham.

The Life Legal Defense Foundation went to bat for Kortney and the Survivors and sued the city of Birmingham. They won the suit, clearing the way for free speech. As one pro-life news source reported,

> In the course of seeking injunctive relief against future interference with the Survivors' right to engage in picketing and leafleting on the public sidewalk, LLDF lawyers learned that the city had a "demonstration" ordinance that required groups as small as two persons to obtain permits before engaging in various free speech activity. . . . This suit not only vindicated the Survivors' rights, but also relieved the local pro-life community of the burden of the onerous law.[2]

The case was *Turn the Hearts v. City of Birmingham.*

During her time with Survivors, Kortney led a team of six to ten young adults, who traveled to 600 high school and college campuses setting up pro-life displays and distributing over 200,000 pieces of educational literature. She mentored dozens of rising pro-life youth at Survivors' annual Pro-life Leadership Training Camps, where she provided hands-on instruction on activist tactics, free speech rights, and defending the pro-life position. She brought her experience and knowledge to Australia in the spring of 2009 with a whirlwind tour of the country that included street activism, training, and an appearance on a local Catholic television program.

After three years with Survivors, Kortney left and returned to the east coast. In June of 2009 she was hired to work as the chapter and street team coordinator for American Life League's Rock for Life project, which brings the human personhood message to youth through music, education, and human rights activism. She was a very welcomed and appreciated activist and was regularly called on to write articles in addition to coordinating and training teams around the country. Her activities also included starting nearly twenty new chapters, frequent blogging on trending pro-life topics, and recording a weekly podcast which was broadcast on National Pro-Life Radio.

In June of 2010, Kortney was hired by Kristan Hawkins of Students for Life of America to work and minister as their field director. Kortney excelled in her new position and quickly began to develop more campus teams all over the country. While at SFLA, she helped start many pro-life groups and received much respect from pro-life students with whom she maintained almost constant contact. Kortney used the knowledge of schools that she gained with Survivors to help students best reach their campuses. She had unique insight into the individual culture that college campuses have.

One of Kortney's favorite things to do with SFLA was teach pro-life apologetics to students. She knew that pro-life students needed to know how to defend their pro-life beliefs clearly and accurately. And she was the perfect person on SFLA staff to do so because of her experience with Survivors and her constant exposure to all things anti-abortion. Kortney was always well-read on the pro-abortion side, kept up with "pro-choice" blogs, and had many books by pro-abortion authors. She knew how to argue for the pro-life side because she knew how the pro-abortion side thought. Kortney flew and drove all over the country, training, equipping, and encouraging student pro-life leaders. She profoundly distinguished herself as an enthusiastic, effective, and inspirational frontrunner of the pro-life movement. And she was a determined and diligent activist who powerfully advanced this great cause while mightily touching the lives of untold numbers of people. Troy Newman, president of Operation Rescue, said of Kortney, ". . . Kortney's life's work stands as a tribute to her warm, loving personality, her fierce dedication to protecting the defenseless, and her unwavering faith in Jesus Christ."[3]

Kortney was a guest speaker at various events, functions, and church groups, such as Charlotte's 40 Days for Life closing celebration and the Los Angeles March for Life. She appeared in publications like North Carolina's *Indy Week* for her protest of the 2008 Democratic National Convention, and on radio programs such as *SoundRezn* and *Giving an Answer*.

During one of her activist adventures, the 2010 March for Life in Washington, D.C., she met Benjamin Gordon, a kindred spirit, pro-life activist, and minister-in-training; the two quickly became good "friends." That summer, at a local waterfall called Welton Falls, Ben got down on one knee and asked her to spend the rest of her life with him, and presented her with a ring. They wed on May 21, 2011. Kortney glowed with a visible radiance of joy and the fairytale wedding was a success.

It didn't come as a big surprise to me when they announced the new life that was created on their honeymoon. Sophy Joy was to be born no later than nine months after their wedding date. Their first five months together were truly times of marital bliss as they planned and prepared for a future together. Kortney was arranging her work schedule so she could back off from some of her travel in preparation for being a new mother. The newlyweds were looking forward to the holidays when they anticipated having more time with each other and with family. But that time of rest and reflection did not come for them.

On October 8, 2011, while she was returning from a Students for Life conference in Georgia, a drunk driver swerved and ran head-on into the car Kortney was driving. She and Sophy, as well as the drunk driver, were killed instantly. Kortney and little Sophy were immediately absent from the body and present with their Lord (2 Cor 5:8). Her three passengers, one in the front seat and two in the back, were critically injured. Her front seat passenger, Jon Scharfenberger, also a pro-life leader and activist with Students for Life of America, died from his injuries ten days later.

A few days after Kortney and Sophy entered eternity, we received the following amazing email from a family who had been at the scene of the accident:

Hello,

My name is Joshua Biron. I was there last night at the scene of the accident. My wife (Ashley Biron) and I came upon the accident no more than thirty seconds after it happened. . . .

My message is this: I came out of my comfort zone to help the five people that were involved in the accident. The other by-standers, seeing my wife and me trying to help, came out of their comfort zones and started helping too. There were fifteen of us working to care for the hurt before EMS and police even showed up. We put ourselves in harm's way to help them. There were men holding the car steady while we pulled people out and away from it. It's time for all of us to come out of our comfort zones. Kortney came out of hers a long time ago. In a world where it seems a lot of people think abortion is OK, she stood against it and gave it her all. There is one thing we can do to keep her awesome spirit alive, and that is for all of you who read this to come out of your comfort zones. To help and support those in need and to stand strong for what is good and right.

The twenty minutes I was at the scene of the accident and then reading Kortney's story today have changed me forever. I hope her story lives on and does the same for more people.

Joshua Biron

We have continued to receive literally hundreds of emails and personal testimonies from many people whose lives Kortney touched. I was already aware of Kortney's incredible influence. What I was not aware of was the inconceivable scope of her impact.

So passionate about the gospel of Jesus Christ, Kortney told her sister Ashley a few weeks before the wreck, "If I knew my death would bring family and friends to Christ, I would gladly lay down my life."

Kortney was a prolific writer who knew what to say and how to say it. Her articles, counsel, and example will continue to have both a temporal and eternal impact. Kortney wrote a powerful article after being deeply moved while visiting the Holocaust Museum; a portion of it is below. Her insightful message to the church and indeed the world is a timeless admonition not to be taken lightly:

. . . Most church leaders do not hesitate when asked to collect food for the homeless or fill shoeboxes for Christmas. But when they're asked to pray outside an abortion mill or allow a pro-life speaker to make a presentation, it's a whole different story. No one gets upset when a church collects a special offering for Haiti, but bring up abortion and you may very well have controversy. So be it. The 50 million children dead from abortion deserve our passion.

In the past, when the body of Christ, the Church, rose up in opposition to an injustice, earth-shaking things happened. Slaves were freed, rights were restored and killings ended.

Sophie Scholl ("The White Rose") asked something that Christians in a country with decriminalized abortion should ask themselves every day: "Who among us has any conception of the dimensions of shame that will befall us and our children when one day the veil has fallen from our eyes and the most horrible of crimes—crimes that infinitely outdistance every human measure—reach the light of day?"[4]

May the Christian churches remove the veil from their eyes and expose the horrible crime against humanity that is abortion. Only then will it end.

16

∽

How Life Connects with Marriage and Family

Bernard and Amber Mauser

Some significant events throughout world history have occurred on January 9th. On this date in 1274, Romeo met Juliet; in 1861, the first shots of the War between the States occurred in South Carolina; in 2007, Steve Jobs revealed the first iPhone; and in 2003, we met for the first time (okay, we made up the Romeo and Juliet account, but the rest is true). You might be thinking, "How can these two people meeting be a significant event in *world* history?" That answer will reveal itself.

Love is a force that naturally desires to increase. People in our society are always saying they are "in love." But as we've learned over the course of our journey together, the power of human love has implications that reach far beyond mere romance or attraction. Love can account for the natural connection between marriage, the sanctity of life, and the importance of the family. When the two of us met, we knew we both cared about the pro-life cause. But we didn't know then how that would come to shape other aspects of our relationship.

Right away we realized how like-minded we were on many essential issues. In fact, less than two weeks after we met I made a very powerful argument to explain why Amber should marry me. I like to tell myself that she must have been persuaded, as we married in December later that year!

When we first met, our shared passion for teaching was revealed when we decided to co-teach the college group at our church. The topic we started with was equipping others to make a comprehensive case for defending the pro-life position. We used the video series *Making Abortion Unthinkable*,[1] along with the books *Politically Correct Death*[2] and *Legislating Morality*.[3] Our hearts were passionate about the pro-life issue.

Despite finding our many areas of agreement, there was one topic about which we differed. This was our different perspectives on children in marriage. I wanted to have a big family; Amber was not excited about the idea. But God had a different plan than anything we imagined.

Conflicting Counsel

After several months, we sought premarital counseling. Godly friends advised us. Everyone said to spend the first year of our marriage really building our relationship. Their consensus was that we ought to use contraception to delay having children during our first years of marriage. There was one couple in our church that challenged this idea. They informed us that some forms of contraception, like the birth control pill, caused abortions. This information threw us for a loop.

Six months later the three of us (me, Amber, and the pill) began our life of wedded bliss, or so we thought. Amber's OB-GYN, who was a Christian, said the pill did not cause abortions. We simply trusted what the physician said. This seemed like a legitimate appeal to authority we could use to answer our friends who insisted otherwise. Nevertheless, we definitely wanted to investigate further just to make sure we were doing the right thing.

After six months of marriage, some friends reiterated what we had previously been told about the pill causing abortions. Upon asking for additional information and documentation, we received some incredible resources. One was a lecture given by Dr. Janet Smith to a Catholic physician's guild titled, "Contraception: Why Not?"[4] The evidence she presented about hormonal birth control was a little overwhelming, but none of it disputed the fact that the pill can cause an early abortion.

Dr. Smith's presentation was persuasive to us as Protestants even though we did not subscribe to what may be considered the "Catholic" elements of her argument. Even more than giving us the medical facts about contraception, her presentation helped us to start thinking about our marriage as an expression of our Christian commitment to life. She introduced us to the idea that intercourse was for babies and bonding.

A Case for Natural Family Planning

The core belief of the pro-life position is that human life should be protected. The Judeo-Christian reason for this position is that life is a gift from God and that we are created in God's image. Taking the life of a human being is an implicit attack on God. The profound value of God's gift calls us to respond to every human person with love rather than violence or fear. The decisions Amber and I made about using contraception came from discovering evidence that bolstered our convictions about the way of living that was most consonant with this message of life. Our research also introduced us to an approach called Natural Family Planning (or NFP for short) that allows married couples to control the size of their family independently.

NFP teaches couples how to accurately keep track of the woman's cycle by paying attention to her fertility signs. As the window of fertility lasts from five days before to one day after a woman ovulates, these natural signs indicate when a woman is fertile. Couples may use NFP as an aid to help them achieve or avoid pregnancy. Right away, it was clear that NFP would be more challenging than the pill. As we learned more about NFP, though, we discovered that there were two different ways of understanding what sex is about. Choosing one over the other would call for major life changes. On the one hand, using NFP would make the natural connection between sex and fertility much more tangible in our day-to-day lives. In order to welcome our fertility as a part of intercourse, we would have to be able to trust one another on a whole new level. Once we realized that conceiving a child is a natural result of having sex, it would become normal to freely share our hopes and burdens about our family. Open dialogue unites us and fortifies our marriage.

As Amber shares with those she counsels, the three areas that couples struggle most with in marriage are sex, money, and children. Following NFP addresses each of these three areas in a way that can strengthen marriage. NFP forces couples to communicate about all of these, deepening their bond and encouraging both partners to make sacrifices for the other.

At the same time that we were learning about the case for NFP, we also discovered that the pill can have serious and dangerous effects. It has been well documented that the birth control pill can have serious effects on a woman's body.[5] The birth control pill works by tricking the woman's body into thinking it is pregnant. Imagine asking the person you love to take a pill that can induce a permanent state of irritability, make them gain weight, and lose sexual desire. This was a lot to ask of Amber in order to ensure that we wouldn't have children. As bad as these side effects are, they are nothing compared to the more serious potential side effects of hormonal birth control.

As fully convinced pro-life advocates, we were really convicted by the fatalities caused by the pill. These deaths have been downplayed in our society (who has ever heard of someone dying from the pill?). We know that every drug has side effects, but we were surprised to learn that the pill sometimes causes blood clotting that can result in a heart attack or a stroke for women who have heart problems. Few speak about the effect the pill has on babies, either. One little-known effect of the pill is that it helps the body stop the newly-formed embryo from being implanted in the case of "break-through" ovulation.[6] If a woman does ovulate and conceive despite being on the pill, her uterus immediately becomes a hostile environment for the embryo. This means that some of the time there is an embryo—a baby—that this pill actively kills.

This information was heart-wrenching as we considered that there was a possibility that, by choosing to use the pill, we may have killed our baby. This guilt caused us to turn to the Lord and seek his grace and forgiveness if, in our ignorance, we had caused this to happen. We found comfort from the Scripture that says, "If we confess our sins, he is faithful and just and will forgive us our sins and purify us from all unrighteousness" (1 John 1:9). We experienced healing from realizing that this revelation from God is based on his unchanging attributes. Much like his covenant with Abraham, God's promise of forgiveness is inviolable; he guarantees our redemption because of his unfailing love and justice.

The pill was promoted as something that could bring us freedom. We had to ask ourselves, freedom from what? At that time, we wanted freedom from having a baby. But it was difficult to consider ourselves to be pro-life without at least being open to new life in our marriage. The word contraception simply means "against conception." What is conception? Well, it's the moment when life begins. With our hearts so devoted to saving and protecting life, we were uncomfortable with practicing something that could blatantly (and in some cases, violently) close us off from life.

Once we realized that using hormonal contraception seemed to contradict our shared commitment to life, we had to ask ourselves why we wanted the total "freedom" promised by the pill. The idea that weighed on us from our research was that we needed to ask ourselves what the natural purpose of sex in marriage was. Why do people have sex? Hollywood portrays it as a self-centered act for instant gratification. However, the purpose of human organs is revealed by their functions. For example, the tongue exists for tasting and the heart for pumping blood. Similarly, one can recognize a purpose for the sexual organs.

What purpose do the sexual organs have for a couple? One purpose is to bond. During stimulation of the sexual organs, both partners release hormones that cause bonding. The male releases vasopressin, which causes him to view the woman differently than other women. This vasopressin hormone in his brain released during intercourse makes him feel "glued" or "bonded" to her.[7] The woman releases oxytocin during intercourse and childbirth which bonds with receptors in her body to produce feelings of intimacy, so she has these feelings for her partner and children.[8] Another purpose of these organs is for a couple to have children. When everything goes right with intercourse—meaning everything works as it should—the result is a child. In sum, babies and bonding are the natural purposes of these organs.

We were able to see how the dual purpose of sex—babies and bonding—is also found in Scripture. In the opening chapters of Genesis, God instructs the first couple to be fruitful and multiply (i.e., have babies). It is also written in the creation account that a man leaves his parents and cleaves to his wife. This unites or bonds them as "one flesh."

Although we had worked through our struggle with the pill, it took us a little more time to reach agreement about whether we should use barrier methods instead. Eventually, however, we both recognized two main reasons for choosing NFP over barrier methods. First, using a barrier still seemed to communicate that we were willing to accept the bonding that comes from intercourse, but not the natural good that comes from fertility. Second, we saw that society promoted barrier methods in a way that devalued many good things which are a product of marital intercourse (e.g., the life of the children who are its natural result).

Our marriage was transformed as these ideas restored meaning and significance to intercourse. Many people say "I want to have sex with you" without any consideration for the entirely natural consequence of this act. It is a completely different thing if a person says, "I want to have children with you." We came to recognize that the separation of these two concepts has trivialized what was once viewed as acceptable only in marriage.

Our Longing for Children

It was not long after this realization that we stopped using contraception. For three long and agonizing years we tried unsuccessfully to start a family. Each month we were met with disappointment. Our friends' delight in becoming pregnant contrasted with our despair. We tried to suppress tears when learning that people who did not want children were now pregnant. Those who viewed children as a burden instead of an incredible gift continued to be blessed while our prayers seemed to go unanswered.

After enduring this struggle for so long, we wrestled with the alternative of seeing a fertility physician. We concluded this would be a wise choice. The doctors ran tests to try to uncover the cause of our infertility and found the problem was with the sperm. The doctor said that apart from some type of intervention we wouldn't be able to have children.

This news came as a tremendous blow. Perhaps it would have been less painful if we hadn't already decided that the forms of intervention that the doctors suggested were immoral. It seemed as though the fulfillment of our longing for a big family was becoming less and less probable. Now it seemed that adoption was our only option. We had to acknowledge that it is God who opens the womb, but we also knew many people whom God did not bless with fertility. We accepted that it may be God's plan for us to be among those he intended to be great adoptive parents.

Answered Prayer

One month after our visit to the fertility doctor—and after being told that we would never be able to conceive children—we discovered that Amber was pregnant! We immediately thought of Abraham and Sarah. God heard our cries and granted us a child. God's grace has been with us not just once, but four times so far! We are so grateful for each of our children.

In the beginning of this story, I mentioned that the day we met was a significant day in world history. It is impossible to over-emphasize that each day of our lives is significant! Human life is imbued with significance because each person is created in God's image. When we came to understand more fully that life is sacred, our marriage was enriched beyond measure, giving us a greater appreciation of the blessings of family. We know from experience that raising children and embracing all that comes from being pro-life is simultaneously the hardest and the easiest way to exhibit God's love.

17

~

One Person, One Group
Can Make a Difference

Dr. Allen D. Unruh

The Declaration of Independence states, in essence, that no human being should be considered mere property to be used, abused, or disposed of at the will of another. Slavery was tolerated at our nation's founding and our nation's bloodiest battle (the Civil War) helped bring about the elimination of slavery. But progress was slow as slavery has been ingrained in cultures for millennia throughout the world. It took the groundwork of people like William Wilberforce in England and Abraham Lincoln in America, who persevered over many years, to eventually win freedom for slaves. It took a hundred years after the civil war for the concept of "separate but equal" to be eliminated by the courts.

One person, with the courage of his or her convictions, can change the course of human history. One small group of people, with biblical convictions, can make a difference. If the whole state of South Dakota were a city, we would still only be the sixty-fifth largest city in America. South Dakota is referred to as a "fly-over" state by some people who live on the east coast. But God has taken a small group of people in a tiny state in the middle of the United States to embolden the entire nation to stand up for life.

There are Christians in South Dakota who are taking decisive action. South Dakota is the only state that has commissioned a task force to study the impact of abortion on this nation. Seventeen people were on this task force who submitted over 3,500 pages of research along with hundreds of testimonies from all over the world. Their research was published as the "Report of the South Dakota Task Force to Study Abortion." The report was so compelling that the South Dakota legislature initially outlawed abortion, with no exceptions except in cases where the life of the mother was threatened. South Dakota is also the only state that has passed the initiative to outlaw abortion twice in the legislature and had it signed into law by the governor. Planned Parenthood, the ACLU, and NARAL immediately took this to the courts.

We have been fighting for life and lost some battles, but South Dakota currently has the strongest pro-life legislation in the nation. The law requires every abortionist to do a thorough history and exam prior to the abortion. The abortionist has to verify that there is no coercion prior to the abortion and there is a required seventy-two-hour waiting period prior to the procedure. Abortionists are required to notify women that they are terminating the life of a separate, unique, living human being. They are also required to notify women that they have a high risk of emotional consequences, including suicide, after an abortion. Women seeking abortions are also required to go to a pregnancy care center prior to an abortion to verify there has been no coercion prior to their decision. One pregnancy center director from Rapid City told the task force that 60 percent of the post-abortive women who received counseling at her center said they had been pressured into aborting against their will.[1]

John Quincy Adams was the only president to run for Congress after serving as president. He ran primarily on one issue: the abolition of slavery. And slavery was such a contentious issue, as abortion is today, that the entire Congress voted to censure him. But he continued to submit legislation anyway. Adams was asked, "Why are you doing this?" He answered, *"Duty is ours; the results are God's."* John Quincy Adams did not live to see the end of slavery, but he became a mentor to a young congressman from Illinois, Abraham Lincoln. We know now that John Quincy Adams was right and the entire Congress was wrong.

History is always influenced by a dedicated minority. That's you and me. Each Christian must now ask themselves, "If not me, who? If not now, when?" Scripture tells us, "From everyone who has been given much, much will be demanded" (Luke 12:48).

My wife Leslee and I received the Salt and Light Award at the Reclaiming America conference for our efforts in getting legislation passed to protect the preborn in South Dakota. Governor Mike Huckabee was the keynote speaker at the conference. Governor Huckabee said he was in Israel and had an opportunity to visit the Holocaust Museum, but he had his eleven-year-old daughter with him. He thought that she was too young to see something this graphic, but he realized that he might never have this opportunity again. He decided that if the exhibits were too hard on her, he would just leave. They walked through the first box car and the stench from that horrendous time still permeated the air. The tour builds in intensity as visitors move past the various exhibits. He held his daughter's hand tightly. They never said a word through the entire two-and-half-hour experience as they read what was at every exhibit. At the end of the tour there was a book for visitors to sign their name and make a comment. He told us, "My daughter stepped up on the step stool and wrote her name and started to write in the comment section."

He thought to himself, "What will she write? She's only eleven years old." He leaned over to watch what she wrote and said, "What she wrote will burn in my heart forever. She wrote five words: 'WHY DIDN'T SOMEBODY DO SOMETHING?'"

Every pro-life advocate and every pregnancy care center is making a contribution toward the destiny of mankind. The time is now to challenge the laws and to help the state of South Dakota take its case to the United States Supreme Court to end this holocaust. The South Dakota Task Force Report is a document like the Declaration of Independence for the unborn. The battle for the preborn and overturning *Roe v. Wade* could come down to the battle lines between Planned Parenthood of South Dakota and Minnesota against the Alpha Center—a pregnancy care center that has had the courage to stand up and be counted in this pivotal time in history. What's at stake? Babies. Families. America. Our entire civilization.

Like William Wilberforce, who fought the slave trade for thirty years, we shall never give up. The legacy of this nation and the lives of countless millions will depend on the courage, under God, of the army of Christians who have committed their lives to this cause. What we are doing makes a difference!

~

Conclusion—Common Threads

Clay Sterrett

We can see some "common threads" in all these of stories—similarities that weave together both the beginnings and the latter parts of their testimonies. These real life stories recount similar experiences of great pain and suffering, and an even greater hope. Every person concerned for the life of the preborn can take courage and learn from their examples. Here are some of the common threads that tie their stories together.

Predicaments

Many of the women and men who contributed to this book began their stories with a seemingly impossible predicament. When she found out that she was pregnant at age seventeen, Jewels Green made plans to raise the child as a single mother—but her hopes were crushed when everyone around her pressured her to have an abortion. She felt abandoned by her family and closest friends. When pastor's son Jon Lineberger learned that his girlfriend was pregnant, he felt trapped by the consequences of his actions. At the time, abortion seemed like the only way out of their predicaments.

Other contributors share that their journey to choosing life began in a time of spiritual crisis. Several of them struggled with the knowledge that they were conceived in rape. One woman realized that her work at Planned Parenthood was wrong, but felt unable to leave the job because she needed the income. For Anthony Horvath and his family, what would normally have been a joyful occasion—his wife's ultrasound at a prenatal checkup—became a time of grieving when they learned that their daughter would be born with spina bifida.

In moments of crisis such as these, choosing life can seem like an impossible burden. But whether our crises are the consequences of our own actions or completely beyond our control, we can be certain that we are never alone. God has promised to help us in our most desperate predicaments. He has promised to be a "refuge and strength, an ever-present help in trouble" for anyone who calls on his name (Ps 46:1). Although many of the stories in this book begin with a crisis, the story doesn't end there.

Hardness of Heart

Many mothers like Jewels Green are coerced into abortion, while others may feel pressured to abort simply because they don't have anyone to support them. But another common thread in these stories is the way that people can suppress the truth and harden their hearts when confronted with the reality and ugliness of abortion.

What does it mean to "harden your heart"? The Bible talks about people who "suppress the truth by their wickedness" and thereby become darkened in their understanding and hardened in heart (Rom 1:18; see also v. 21). We are warned in Scripture not to become "hardened by sin's deceitfulness" (Heb 3:13). Nowhere is this more apparent than in those who insist on being "pro-choice" despite what is revealed by science and ultrasound technology—it is a *human*, a real *person,* an innocent *baby* in the womb who is being considered for abortion. But the real problem isn't that abortion supporters don't have the facts—it's that they haven't taken the grave human consequences of abortion to heart.

As these stories show, men and women can be hardened against the truth about abortion—that it takes the life of a pre-born human child—for many different reasons. One professor who enjoyed his sexual freedom admitted that he "took the easy way out" and "adopted the bland assertions of pro-choice advocates who claimed that the pre-born were not human" in order to justify his irresponsible lifestyle. Others may even recognize the humanity of the pre-born child, but still choose to support abortion. Jewels' description of her sudden change into "a die-hard, closed-minded abortion rights advocate" in order to push away her grief and guilt shows how painful the truth about abortion is, even for those who are avowedly "pro-choice." Even when people recognize abortion for what it is, they can still close their hearts to the demands that truth places on their lives. As former Planned Parenthood employee Ramona Treviño's story shows, it can even be easy to drown out the voice of conscience with our own good intentions. After referring a patient for an abortion, she shares, "I knew I had done something wrong. Yet my mind began the justification. I remember wiping my tears away and saying to myself, *'This decision is hers. I'm not here to judge anyone. Besides, this is between her and God.'*"

One Person Makes a Difference

What changes a hardened heart? In each of the stories where a person made a moral and mental turnaround on the abortion issue, there was often one person in particular who helped by reaching out and encouraging them to make the right decision. In some cases, this meant sharing the sobering truth about the abortion procedure. It didn't take much to make a difference. In one case, a professor found himself confronted by an old friend who challenged his liberal views on abortion. In fifteen minutes, she gave him some ideas he could not shake from his mind. He said her simple focus on the key issue was like a "stone in his shoe."

In many other stories, one person made a difference simply by reaching out with love. A man who encouraged the abortion of his own child was brought to repentance through his parents' dedicated prayers. Others found hope through the loving persistence of complete strangers, sidewalk counselors and pregnancy care workers. Lauren Muzyka's beautiful story about meeting a woman and her pregnant daughter outside an abortion clinic perfectly captures the way that these ordinary men and women can transform the life of a person in crisis. As they talked, Lauren writes, "this young mother began to see how it was possible—even wonderful—for her to choose life." Simply offering loving support to a person in crisis can make what seemed like an impossible burden into a wonderful gift.

Each of the stories in this book attests to the fact that God uses ordinary people—mostly in one-on-one situations—to soften hearts that are hardened by sin and affect people for his kingdom. He can use us, but we need to be available. Is there anyone we could be reaching out to right now?

We must also remember that no one is ever too far gone to be reached by the grace of God. Jesus's disciple Peter wrote, "The Lord is . . . patient with you, not wanting anyone to perish, but everyone to come to repentance" (2 Pet 3:9). We should not hesitate to speak up because we are afraid of being rejected. By reaching out with love, we can share our conviction that there is no heart too hard to be changed by the truth.

A Change of Mind

Many of the formerly "pro-choice" people in our stories had a change of mind. The truth about the preborn finally convinced them. Although she was already volunteering for a pregnancy care center, Kristan Hawkins reached a turning point when she watched videos that showed the gruesome effects of abortion. All she could think was, "How could anyone see and grasp what abortion really is and not do everything within their power to stop it?" At that moment, the conclusion that abortion kills a human being finally hit home—and she knew she had to do something.

Jewels Green's "aha moment" came when she heard about a child who was aborted because he had Down Syndrome. After that, she writes, "My mental attitude shifted completely and I finally (finally!) understood: abortion kills an innocent human being . . . every time. I was now pro-life. My whole worldview shifted 180 degrees." Stories like hers are proof that, as she writes, "conversion is real—and possible."

The Christian life begins with the words, "Repent and believe the good news!" (Mark 1:15). To follow Christ, we must have a "change of mind"—turning away from a self-centered viewpoint to a God-centered viewpoint. We must also believe the good news about Christ's death and resurrection. All through life, we must be continually "transformed through the renewing of our minds" (Rom 12:2). This renewing of our minds affects *every* area of life and certainly includes thinking God's way about life-and-death issues.

Being pro-life always requires that we draw close to Christ and bring others to him, so that he can continue to transform our hearts and minds. Many of our authors described their "change of mind" about abortion as a moment of conversion and reconciliation to God. As Carmen Pate writes, "I knew my life was different when my eyes were opened to the truth about the sin of abortion. . . . When God saved me I knew I had been forgiven, because I felt free for the first time in my life."

Discovering God's Incredible Forgiveness

Those who have chosen abortion often live with incredible guilt and regret about their decision. One of the greatest truths in the Bible is that there is no sin too big to be covered by the shed blood of Christ. We can be certain that "if we confess our sins, he is faithful and just and will forgive us our sins and purify us from all unrighteousness" (1 John 1:9). Each of our writers could testify of this wonderful gift of forgiveness. Jon Lineberger writes,

> I never felt that I deserved to get married, let alone to have my own children, because of the way I had treated women in past relationships. But in God's grace "deserving" has nothing to do with it. God has blessed me with a beautiful, forgiving wife and three wonderful children. God forgives us and showers grace and mercy upon us because of the sacrifice of Jesus Christ. In return God only asks that we submit our lives to him.
>
> King David was someone who knew of God's grace and mercy first hand. He had sinned greatly, but he had also experienced God's great forgiveness. This David, a forgiven sinner like me, wrote, "as far as the east is from the west, so far has he removed our transgressions from us. As a father has compassion on his children, so the LORD has compassion on those who fear him" (Ps 103:12-13).

Nothing—not even abortion—can exhaust God's compassion for his children. Regardless of what we have done, the fact remains that he created us to share his joy. Whenever we turn to him with our guilt, sin, and heartache, he will not hesitate to set us free and restore us to life in him. The tremendous redemption he has given us in Christ can make us able to say, in the words of one author:

Having been redeemed and set free from the shackles of my sin, I refuse to simply wear the label "post-abortive woman." I am a child of the King of kings, who has been forgiven much for the sin of abortion, as well as many other sins. God continues to heal and restore my life as his Spirit works to transform me into Christ's likeness. . . . Perhaps through me, God may display his perfect patience, so that others may believe and receive eternal life.

Now Pro-Life: Ordinary People Making a Difference

The Bible is a record of ordinary people who were used by an extraordinary God to impact the world with his love and message of truth. In our stories, we've seen that the pro-life movement has produced a great host of ordinary people, now transformed in their thinking, who are speaking out for the cause of Christ and defending those who cannot speak out for themselves. Some of their actions may seem rather simple, but if we multiply these efforts by a thousand, it makes a difference. We have seen a former atheist, now a pro-life activist, who challenges college students to define life while using logic and scientific studies to support his pro-life position. Other pro-life activists are students themselves, who organize pro-life groups on high school and college campuses and bring their convictions to their classrooms. We've heard from one woman who hosts a radio talk show that promotes the sanctity of life—and another whose decision to quit her job at Planned Parenthood was first sparked when she happened to tune in to a pro-life program.

We've seen everyday people who seek to heal the hurt of abortion in many different ways, from sidewalk counseling and praying outside clinics to leading men's post-abortion recovery groups and connecting abortion survivors in a network of support. Others found new ways to bring the message of life into their own homes, transforming their understanding of marriage and parenthood to reflect the dignity of the preborn. Many others have contributed to what is perhaps the simplest but most necessary task: supporting a local pro-life pregnancy help center.

We close with these encouraging words from two of our contributors:

> Please understand that he took a very ordinary, broken vessel, one who was willing to be led by his hand, and to be used by him for life. . . . We are all in the "lifesaving" business, and though God may place you in different circles of influence than mine, there will always be a life that is waiting for his touch through you. May he find each of us faithful to reach out to the least among us with the same compassion we have been shown.

> One thing is evident: the salvation and restoration of sinful people is God's work. It is even more mind-boggling to think that he uses people like you and me to help in the process of healing others and to execute his will on earth. If God can save and use a man like me, there is hope for any man!

~

Appendix—How to Make a Case for Life in Five Minutes or Less[1]

Scott Klusendorf

You don't need a doctoral degree to be persuasive as you defend your pro-life views. You just need clarity.

Suppose that you have just five minutes to graciously defend your pro-life beliefs with friends or clients. Can you do it with rational arguments? What should you say? And how can you begin simplifying the abortion issue for those who think it's hopelessly complex?

True, every conversation is different, but here are three general steps that will enable you to engage your listener:

Clarify the issue. Pro-life advocates contend that elective abortion unjustly takes the life of a defenseless human being. This simplifies the abortion controversy by focusing public attention on just one question: Is the preborn a member of the human family? If so, killing him or her to benefit others is a serious moral wrong. It treats the distinct human being, who has his or her own inherent moral worth, as no more than a disposable instrument. Conversely, of course, if the preborn are not human, killing them for any reason requires no more justification than having a tooth pulled.

In other words, arguments based on "choice" or "privacy" miss the point entirely. Would anyone that you know support a mother killing her toddler in the name of "choice" and "the right to decide"? Clearly, if the preborn are human like toddlers, we shouldn't kill them in the name of choice anymore than we would a toddler. Again, this debate is about just one question: what is the unborn child? At this point, some may object that your comparisons are not fair—that killing a fetus is morally different from killing a toddler. Ah, but that's the issue, isn't it? Are the unborn, like toddlers, members of the human family? *That is the one issue that matters.*

Remind your conversation partner that you are vigorously "pro-choice" when it comes to women choosing a number of moral goods. You support a woman's right to choose her own doctor, to choose her own partner, to choose her own job, and to choose her own religion, to name a few. These are among the many choices that you fully support for women. But some choices are wrong, like killing innocent human beings simply because they are in the way and cannot defend themselves.[2] We shouldn't be allowed to choose that.

Defend your pro-life position with science and philosophy. The science of embryology tells us that from the earliest stages of development, the preborn are distinct, living, and whole human beings. Leading embryology studies confirm this.[3] For example, Keith L. Moore and T. V. N. Persaud write that "A zygote is the beginning of a new human being. Human development begins at fertilization, the process during which a male gamete or sperm . . . unites with a female gamete or oocyte . . . to form a single cell called a zygote. This highly specialized, totipotent cell marks the beginning of each of us as a unique individual."[4] Prior to his abortion advocacy, former Planned Parenthood president Dr. Alan Guttmacher was perplexed that anyone, much less a medical doctor, would question this. "This all seems so simple and evident that it is difficult to picture a time when it wasn't part of the common knowledge," he wrote in his book *Life in the Making.*[5]

Philosophically, while it's true that embryos are less developed than newborns (or, for that matter, toddlers), this difference is not morally significant in the way abortion advocates need it to be. Consider the claim that the immediate capacity for self-awareness bestows value on human beings. Notice that this is not an argument, but an arbitrary assertion. Why is some development needed? And why is this particular degree of development (i.e., higher brain function) decisive rather than another? These are questions that abortion advocates do not adequately address.

As Stephen Schwarz points out, there is no morally significant difference between the embryo that you once were and the adult that you are today that would justify killing you at that early stage of development. Differences of size, level of development, environment, and degree of dependency between an embryo and an adult would not be enough to justify the claim that you had no rights as an embryo but you do have rights today.[6] Think of the acronym SLED as a helpful reminder of these non-essential differences:

SIZE: True, embryos are smaller than newborns and adults, but why is that relevant? Do we really want to say that large people are more human than small ones? Men are generally larger than women, but that doesn't mean that they deserve more rights. Size doesn't equal value.

LEVEL OF DEVELOPMENT: True, embryos and fetuses are less developed than the adults they'll one day become. But again, why is this relevant? Four-year-old girls are less developed than fourteen-year-old ones. Should older children have more rights than their younger siblings? Some people say that self-awareness makes one human. But if that is true, newborns do not qualify as valuable human beings. Six-week-old infants lack the immediate capacity for performing human mental functions, as do the reversibly comatose, the sleeping, and those with Alzheimer's Disease.

ENVIRONMENT: Where you are has no bearing on who you are. Does your value change when you cross the street or roll over in bed? If not, how can a journey of eight inches down the birth canal suddenly change the essential nature of the preborn from non-human to human? If the preborn are not already human, merely changing their location can't make them valuable.

DEGREE OF DEPENDENCY: If viability makes us human, then all those who depend on insulin or kidney medication are not valuable and we may kill them. Conjoined twins who share blood type and bodily systems also have no right to life under this argument. In short, it's far more reasonable to argue that although humans differ immensely with respect to talents, accomplishments, and degrees of development, they are nonetheless equal because they share a common human nature.

Challenge your listeners to be intellectually honest. Ask the tough questions. When critics say that birth makes the preborn human, ask, "How does a mere change of location from inside the womb to outside the womb change the essential nature of the unborn?" If they say that brain development or self-awareness makes us human, ask if they would agree that those with an IQ below 40 or perhaps 60 should be declared non-persons? If not, why not? True, some people will ignore the scientific and philosophic case you present for the pro-life view and argue for abortion based on self-interest. That is the lazy way out. Remind your critics that if we care about truth, we will courageously follow a good argument wherever it leads, no matter what the cost to our own self-interests.

Finally, let's toughen the job. Suppose you only get one minute to make your pro-life case. Frame the issue this way: Either you believe that each and every human being has an equal right to life or you don't. The science of embryology tells us that from the earliest stages of development, the preborn are distinct, living, and whole human beings. Sure, they have yet to mature, but they are whole human beings just the same. Philosophically, there is no essential difference between the embryo you once were and the adult you are today that would justify killing you at that earlier stage. Differences of size, level of development, environment, and degree of dependency are not good reasons for saying you could be killed then but not now.

Notes

Notes to Introduction

1. Jim Douglas, "Abortion doctor: 'Am I killing? Yes, I am,'" YouTube video, from a segment aired on KVUE News, posted by "CreativeMinority," November 6, 2009, https://www.youtube.com/watch?v=bfWB7tcAdhw; see also Dr. Susan Berry, "New Mexico Abortionist: 'Am I Killing? Yes, I Am,'" Breitbart, May 13, 2013, http://www.breitbart.com/Big-Government/2013/05/10/Abortionist-in-Albuquerque-NM-Clinic-Am-I-killing-Yes-I-Am.

2. Erwin W. Lutzer, *When a Nation Forgets God: 7 Lessons We Must Learn from Nazi Germany* (Chicago: Moody Publishers, 2010), 21–22.

3. David Bereit paraphrasing G. Frederick Owen, *Abraham Lincoln: The Man and His Faith* (Wheaton, IL: Tyndale, 1981).

4. Frederick Douglass, *Narrative of the Life of Frederick Douglass, An American Slave* (Boston: Anti-Slavery Office, 1845; University Library, The University of North Carolina at Chapel Hill, 1999), 119, http://docsouth.unc.edu/neh/douglass/douglass.html.

5. "The top 10 causes of death," May, 2014, World Health Organization, http://www.who.int/mediacentre/factsheets/fs310/en/.

6. "Numbers of Abortions," http://www.numberofabortions.com/. See also "Abortion: Worldwide Levels and Trends," Gilda Sedgh, Guttmacher Institute, 2007, http://www.guttmacher.org/presentations/AWWtrends.html.

7. Mother Teresa of Calcutta, "Whatsoever You Do . . . : Speech of Mother Teresa of Calcutta to the National Prayer Breakfast, Washington, D.C., February 3, 1994," Priests for Life, http://www.priestsforlife.org/brochures/mtspeech.html.

8. Abby Johnson, *Unplanned* (Carol Stream, IL: Tyndale House Publishers, 2011), 5.

9. *Pain-Capable Unborn Child Protection Act of 2013: Hearings on H. R. 1797,* 113th Cong. (2013) (written statement of Dr. Anthony Levatino), http://thomas.loc.gov/cgi-bin/cpquery/?&sid=cp113MHseG&r_n=hr109p1.113&d bname=cp113&&sel=TOC_14230&, accessed on June 5, 2015.

Notes to Chapter 6: Sidewalk Counseling

1. This chapter was originally published online as "Lauren's Story: An Adventure I Never Expected," Sidewalk Advocates for Life, December 17, 2013, http://sidewalkadvocates.org/laurens-story-an -adventure-i-never-expected-part-i/ and http://sidewalkadvocates.org/ laurens-story-an-adventure-i-never-expected-part-ii/#more-199.

Notes to Chapter 15: Abortion Abolitionist

1. Erik Whittington, "In Kortney Blythe Gordon, We Have Lost a Loved One," LifeNews.com, October 10, 2011 http://www.lifenews.com/2011/10/10/ in-kortney-blythe-gordon-we-have-lost-a-loved-one/.

2. Steven Ertelt, "Birmingham Alabama Settles Lawsuit With Pro-Lifers Denied Free Speech," LifeNews.com, November 10, 2010, www.lifenews .com/2010/11/10/state-5660/?pr=1.

3. "Kortney Blythe Gordon Named Operation Rescue's 2011 Pro-life Person of the Year," ChristianNewsWire, December 29, 2011, www.christiannewswire .com/news/4491318546.html.

4. Kortney Blythe Gordon, "Remembering the Holocaust," American Life League, March 19, 2010, http://www.all.org/article/index/id/NjIzMg. In this article, Kortney also comments: "If you've never heard of Sophie Scholl and The White Rose, look it up or rent the movie *Sophie Scholl: The Final Days.* Sophie and her brother, Hans, were college students compelled by their Christian faith to speak out against Hitler and the Nazi agenda through non-violent means. Their leaflets influenced thousands, and they were martyred for their courage. They quoted extensively from the Bible and unequivocally challenged people to wake up from their indifferent slumber."

Notes to Chapter 16: How Life Connects

1. Gregory Koukl and Scott Klusendorf, *Making Abortion Unthinkable: The Art of Pro-Life Persuasion,* Stand to Reason Interactive Series (Stand To Reason, date unknown), DVD.

2. Francis Beckwith, *Politically Correct Death: Answering Arguments for Abortion Rights* (Grand Rapids: Baker Books, 1993).

3. Norman L. Geisler and Frank Turek, *Legislating Morality: Is It Wise? Is It Legal? Is It Possible?* (Minneapolis: Bethany House Publishers, 1998).

4. Janet E. Smith, "Contraception: Why Not?," address to a Catholic Physician's Guild Meeting at the Pontifical College Josephinum in Columbus, Ohio in May 1994. See also Janet E. Smith, *Contraception: Why Not?* (Dayton, OH: One More Soul, 2004), DVD.

5. For general information about the effects of the pill, see The American Society of Health-System Pharmacists, Inc., "Estrogen and Progestin (Oral Contraceptives)," U. S. Library of Medicine, 2015, https://www.nlm.nih.gov/medlineplus/druginfo/meds/a601050.html#side-effects. The leading medical journals in the world have also corroborated the dangers of the pill with numerous studies. Taking the pill doubles the risk of heart attack and can cause blood clots (B. C. Tanis et al., "Oral Contraceptives and the Risk of Myocardial Infarction," *NEJM* 345, no. 25 [2001]: 1787–93). Women who use the pill are more than three times more likely to develop breast cancer (Jessica M. Dolle et al., "Risk Factors for Triple-Negative Breast Cancer in Women Under the Age of 45 Years," *Cancer Epidemiology, Biomarkers & Prevention* 18, no. 4 [2009]: 1157–65). Women are also significantly more likely to develop liver and cervical cancers in addition to infections from taking the pill (Chia C. Wang et al., "Risk of HIV Infection in Oral Contraceptive Pill Users: A Meta-analysis," *JAIDS* 21, 1 [1999]: 51–58; *Combined Estrogen-Progestogen Contraceptives, IARC* Monograph 91 [2007]; Victor Moreno et al., "Effect of Oral Contraceptives on Risk of Cervical Cancer in Women with Human Papillomavirus Infection," *Lancet* 359, 9312 [March 30, 2002]: 1085–92).

6. "Proof that break-through ovulation (sometimes also called 'escape-ovulation') does occur even under perfect health conditions was first shown by Dr. Nine Van der Vange, State University of Utrecht, The Netherlands, Dept. of Obstetrics & Gynaecology in 1984. Dr. Van der Vange's research used high resolution ultrasound which visually showed that women ovulate on the popularly prescribed low dose pill. A blood test confirmed that ovulation had occurred. The pill can have a break-through ovulation rate that can be as high as 17 ovulations per 100 women who used the pill for one year. Other researchers have shown that the low dose pill has an even higher rate of break-through ovulation of almost 27 ovulations per 100 women per year" (John Wilks, "The Pill: How it Works and Fails," lifeissues.net, 2000, http://www.pfli.org/faq_oc.html).

7. Ed Vitagliano, "Bonded in the Brain: New Science Confirms the Biblical View of Sex," *AFA Journal*, October 2010, 14-15: http://www.ruthinstitute.org/ITAF11/reading/bondedInBrain_v2.pdf; Marla V. Broadfoot, "High On Fidelity," *American Scientist*, May-June 2002, https://www.americanscientist.org/issues/pub/high-on-fidelity.

8. Ibid.

Notes to Chapter 17: One Person, One Group

1. "Report of the South Dakota Task Force to Study Abortion," December 2005, p. 21, http://www.dakotavoice.com/Docs/South%20Dakota%20Abortion%20Task%20Force%20Report.pdf.

Notes to Appendix

1. This appendix was originally published online as "The Five-Minute Pro-Lifer," Life Training Institute, http://prolifetraining.com/wp-content/uploads/2014/02/FiveMinute1.pdf.

2. For more on this, see Gregory Koukl, *Precious Preborn Human Persons* (Lomita: STR Press, 1999), 11.

3. See T. W. Sadler, *Langman's Embryology*, 5th ed. (Philadelphia: W. B. Saunders, 1993), 3; Ronand O'Rahilly and Pabiola Muller, *Human Embryology and Teratology*, 2nd ed. (New York: Wiley-Liss, 1996), 8, 29.

4. Keith L. Moore and T. V. N. Persaud, *The Developing Human: Clinically Oriented Embryology* (Philadelphia: W. B. Saunders Company, 1998), 2.

5. A. Guttmacher, *Life in the Making: The Story of Human Procreation* (New York: Viking Press, 1933), 3.

6. Stephen Schwarz, *The Moral Question of Abortion* (Chicago: Loyola University Press, 1990), 18.